THE ANALYTICAL DIDACTIC
OF COMENIUS

THE ANALYTICAL DIDACTIC
OF COMENIUS

[JAN AMOS KOMENSKÝ]

Translated
from the Latin with Introduction and Notes by

VLADIMIR JELINEK

THE UNIVERSITY OF CHICAGO PRESS

THIS FIRST ENGLISH EDITION OF COMENIUS'

Analytical Didactic

IS A COMMEMORATIVE VOLUME IN CELEBRATION

OF THE CENTENNIAL ANNIVERSARY OF

WASHINGTON UNIVERSITY

WHICH AIDED IN THE PUBLICATION

OF THIS WORK

THE UNIVERSITY OF CHICAGO PRESS, CHICAGO 37

CAMBRIDGE UNIVERSITY PRESS, LONDON, N.W. 1, ENGLAND

Mým prvním učitelům, otci a matce

PREFACE

JAN AMOS KOMENSKÝ (COMENIUS) wrote three general treatises on didactic method; these works, in order of their composition, are the Czech *Didaktika*, the Latin *Didactica magna*, and the tenth chapter of the Latin *Linguarum methodus novissima*, a chapter to which Czech publications commonly refer as *Didaktika analytická (Analytical Didactic)*. The *Didactica magna*, which is virtually a translation of the Czech *Didaktika*, has been rendered into English by M. W. Keatinge in his excellent translation and commentary entitled *The Great Didactic*, but the *Analytical Didactic* has never before appeared in English. The present volume, which contains the first English translation of Comenius' third and last didactic, provides a version of the text in the first edition of the *Methodus* (1648/9) and indicates significant revisions and additions made by Comenius in the second edition (1657).

In the *Methodus*, of which the *Analytical Didactic* is the kernel, Comenius shows the growing influence of his preoccupation with pansophy; although he continues to expound the central ideas of his earlier works on education, he abandons the very principles and techniques which had made those works (e.g., the *Ianua*) famous throughout Europe. Discarding the analogical method of the Czech and Latin didactics, he substitutes for it a rigid system of definition, analysis, and deduction. Hence the *Analytical Didactic* becomes a major document in the intellectual history of Comenius.

In the extensive and polyglot literature on Comenius there is no thorough study of the variations on the major themes enunciated in the three didactics. The present volume is intended as a contribution to such a study; besides providing an English text of the last didactic, it attempts, by means of notes and general comments, to furnish materials for an examination of the author's changing theories of method. Students of education may also find this work a useful document in the history of pedagogical theory as it evolves from Vives through Ratke and Comenius to the moderns. My commentary, however, is chiefly designed to point up the relations of Comenius' thinking to the intellectual life of the seventeenth century, particularly to Baconian, pansophic, irenic, and chiliastic fashions of thought.

In order to place the *Analytica* within its proper setting, the Introduction supplies an outline of the thirty chapters of the *Methodus*, the space allotted to any given chapter being determined partly by the relative importance of the material and partly by special considerations. Chapter viii, for instance, is treated rather fully because it contains a survey of Renaissance theories of language study and also because it discusses authors whose works are inaccessible or not readily available; hence the numerous footnotes, which supply biographical and bibliographical information difficult to find even in specialized reference works.

To facilitate comparison between the *Analytical Didactic* and the *Great Didactic*, Appendix I furnishes an outline of the leading principles formulated in the two works. Appendix II describes the earlier plan of the textbooks that Comenius rewrote in order to make them conform to the theories developed in the *Methodus*. Appendix III gives a short account of the recent discovery of the works in which Comenius summed up the pansophic theories and schemes that dominated the writings of his mature years.

Comenian studies written in English, though extensive and often highly informative, derive largely from German studies, the contributions of M. Spinka and O. Odložilík being notable exceptions. Because of the barriers of language, which Comenius endeavored to break down, Czech scholarship usually reaches English and American students through indirect channels or not at all. The kindness of friends in Czechoslovakia has provided me with books that made it possible to base the present translation and commentary on the learned publications of Czech scholars, particularly E. Čapek, J. Hendrich, J. V. Novák, J. Reber, and B. Ryba.

Acknowledgment of great indebtedness is due to the members of the Central Administration of Washington University, Chancellor Arthur H. Compton, former Dean Edward K. Graham (now chancellor of the Woman's College of the University of North Carolina), Dean Thomas S. Hall, and Dean Carl Tolman, who granted me leave of absence to complete this work. Professor Guy A. Cardwell gave me generously of his time and unfailingly supplied me with expert criticism and kindly advice. Dr. D. K. Colville helped me with revision and proofreading. Without the gracious and liberal aid of Jan Vaňous, Miloš Jelínek, and Marie Kroutilová, who parted with irreplaceable volumes in order to speed my work, I should have been unable to consult indispensable books. Agnes M. Jelinek lightened my task immeasurably by devoting more than two years to painstaking research and detailed criticism of every page of this volume. Finally, my thanks must go to my parents, who taught me the language of Komenský.

V. J.

St. Louis, Missouri
August 1951

CONTENTS

ABBREVIATIONS

Analytica *Didactica analytica*, the tenth chapter of the *Linguarum methodus novissima.*

Archiv *Archiv pro bádání o životě a spisech J. A. Komenského* ("Archive for Research in the Life and Works of J. A. Komenský"). Brno, 1910–40.

KEATINGE M. W. KEATINGE. *The Great Didactic of John Amos Comenius.* 2 vols. London, 1896; 2d ed., 1907; enlarged 2d ed., 1910; reprinted, 1921.

Methodus *Linguarum methodus novissima.* (*S.l., s.a.*) Published in Leszno in 1648 or 1649. Republished as *Methodus linguarum novissima* in *ODO*, II, 1–292.

MCG *Monatshefte der Comenius-Gesellschaft.* Leipzig [*et al.*]. 1892——.

NOVÁK-HENDRICH JAN V. NOVÁK and JOSEF HENDRICH. *Jan Amos Komenský: Jeho život a spisy* ("J. A. Komenský: His Life and Works"). Praha, 1932.

ODO *Jani Comenii Opera didactica omnia.* 4 vols. Amsterdam, 1657 [1657–58].

REBER JOSEF REBER and JAN V. NOVÁK (eds.). *Linguarum methodus novissima* in *VSJAK*, VI, Part II (1911), 183–530.

SPEDDING JAMES SPEDDING, R. L. ELLIS, and D. D. HEATH (eds.). *Works of Francis Bacon.* 14 vols. London, 1857–74.

SPINKA

MATTHEW SPINKA. *John Amos Comenius: That Incomparable Moravian.* Chicago, 1943.

VSJAK

Veškeré spisy Jana Amosa Komenského ("The Collected Works of J. A. Komenský"), published by the Ústřední Spolek Jednot Učitelských na Moravě. Brno, 1911–26.

BIBLIOGRAPHICAL NOTES

A. THE TEXT OF THE "ANALYTICAL DIDACTIC"

The *Linguarum methodus novissima,* the tenth chapter of which constitutes the *Analytical Didactic,* appeared in two editions during the lifetime of Comenius. The first edition, entitled *Linguarum methodus novissima,* is an octavo volume of 688 pages printed in Leszno by Daniel Vetter in 1649; its title-page gives no indication of place, time, or printer but is adorned with Comenius' favorite motto: *Absit violentia rebus. Omnia sponte fluant* ("Let violence be absent. Let all things flow spontaneously"). The Dedication, addressed to Ludovic de Geer, is "sent from Elbing in Prussia . . . toward the close of the year 1648."

In the second edition the order of the words in the title is changed to *Novissima linguarum methodus,* and the text is slightly expanded. This revised version was first printed in the folio edition of Comenius' *Opera didactica omnia* (Amsterdam, 1657), II, 1–292; it lacks the valuable thirty-eight-page Index of the first edition but supplies a brief outline for the tenth chapter of the *Methodus.*

The present translation is made from the Latin text of the first edition as edited, with variants and additions from the second edition, by Josef Reber and Jan V. Novák in *Veškeré spisy Jana Amosa Komenského* ("The Collected Works of Jan Amos Komenský"), published by the Ústřední Spolek Jednot Učitelských na Moravě (Brno, 1911), VI, Part II, 183–556. References to this edition are marked "Reber."

B. GENERAL BIBLIOGRAPHY

No complete list of Comenius' writings can ever be compiled because a large part of his correspondence, many of his manuscript works, and even some of his published books are irretrievably lost. Discoveries like those of Čyževskij, noted in Appendix III below, cannot restore works which are known to have perished through fire or wanton destruction. Many of Comenius' messages, especially secret political notes sent by private courier, can never be recovered.

Of the more than two hundred works that Comenius finished, left incomplete, or planned to write, more than one hundred and fifty are now extant, two-thirds of these being in Latin. Even the modern reprints of some of these works are at present difficult of access. The body of international literature dealing with Comenius remains an uncatalogued mass. The most comprehensive survey of works by and about Comenius, although it extends only to the year 1911, lists 13,300 items: Čeněk Zíbrt, *Bibliografie české historie* ("Bibliography of Czech History") (Praha, 1910–12), V, 325–650. Supplementing the work of Zíbrt and providing the most recent general review of Comenian studies is the bibliographical section in Jan Jakubec, *Dějiny literatury české* ("History of Czech Literature") (2d ed.; Praha, 1929), Volume I. The work of Novák-Hendrich contains the most extensive collection of materials for the study of Comenius' life and a detailed analysis of his writings; Hendrich, whose continuation of Novák's work begins on page 627, supplies an invaluable descriptive bibliography and a useful index. Bibliographical notices of Comeniana appear in various philological and pedagogical journals, the most useful of these being the *Archiv*, which is devoted exclusively to Comenian studies; unfortunately, no issues of the *Archiv* have appeared since 1940.

Among recent and readily accessible general studies of Comenius the most useful is Anna Heyberger's *Jean Amos Comenius: Sa vie et son œuvre d'éducateur* (Paris, 1928), pages 243–65 of which contain a selective bibliography notable for its accurate information about title-pages. In English a valuable introduction to Comenian studies is Spinka's book, which utilizes the results of modern Czech scholarship; Spinka's bibliography (pp. 156–70), which lists only extant works, is especially helpful as a guide to the study of irenic movements in England and on the Continent. Keatinge (II, 309–16) records extant and nonextant works, but some of his dates need revising. Pages 440–49 of G. H. Turnbull's *Hartlib, Dury and Comenius* (London: University

Press of Liverpool [Hodder & Stoughton], 1947) contain a valuable list of Comenius' works as they are recorded in contemporary correspondence.

Almost all the extant correspondence of Comenius is to be found in A. Patera's *J. A. Komenského korrespondence* (Praha, 1892) and in Jan Kvačala's two collections: *Korrespondence J. A. Komenského* (2 vols.; Praha, 1897 and 1902) and *Analecta Comeniana* (Jurjev, 1909).

The most scholarly modern editions of Comenius' writings are published in the monumental *VSJAK*, each volume being provided with a full critical apparatus. The editors of this series had intended to print the complete works of Comenius in thirty volumes, but from 1911 to 1926 they completed only about one-fourth of the project; no new volumes have been added since 1926.

The publishing association of scholars known as Dědictví Komenského / Héritage de Coménius / Comenius-Erbschaft was recently dissolved, its functions being taken over in part by the Státní Pedagogické Nakladatelství (State Pedagogical Publishing House) in Praha. This new organization has promised a new and complete edition of all the didactic works of Comenius. In January, 1952, it inaugurated what it calls a "New Series of the Dědictví Komenského" by publishing, under the editorship of F. R. Tichý, *J. A. Komenský: Didaktické spisy*. This volume contains modern Czech versions of the Czech *Didaktika*, the *Analytical Didactic*, the *Informatorium*, the *Paradisus Bohemiae (Ráj český)*, and the *Navržení krátké*, but only portions of the *Didactica magna*. There are also plans, as yet ill defined, to continue the *VSJAK* in editions that will reproduce the original language of the texts and supply modern Czech translations on the same page.

INTRODUCTION

I

PRELIMINARY REMARKS

THE *Analytical Didactic* (*Didaktika analytická*) is a title that has been commonly applied by Czech scholars to the tenth chapter of the *Linguarum methodus novissima* of Comenius ever since F. J. Zoubek's translation of that chapter was so entitled when published as a separate work in 1874.[1] Comenius himself gave no special heading to this portion of his work, nor did he ever print it separately; but he does call particular attention to it as a fundamental departure from his earlier theories of how a didactic should be constructed.[2] This "new" didactic, elaborated in the longest chapter of his "newest" method, constitutes so important an innovation in the author's treatment of didactic technique that modern scholars have come to regard it as the third and last didactic of Comenius. The first of these didactics, the Czech *Didaktika*, discovered in Leszno in 1841 and published by V. Tomek in 1849, was composed between 1628 and 1632. The Latin *Didactica magna*, although not published until 1657, was written between 1633 and 1638. Thus in point of composition the *Analytical Didactic*, which appeared in the *Linguarum methodus novissima* of 1649 and was composed between 1644 and 1647, represents the last of the author's attempts at a general formulation of didactic technique. It also embodies an entirely new approach to the subject, an analytical and deductive treatment foreign to the two earlier works.

Although most of the leading ideas in the three didactics

1. Published in Praha by the Beseda Učitelská.
2. Cf. the second (Amsterdam) edition of the *Methodus*, chap. ix, last par.

are fundamentally the same, the rigorously analytic and deductive treatment of these ideas in the *Analytica* contrasts sharply with the comparative and analogical method of the Czech *Didaktika* and the *Didactica magna*.[3] Intended as a formulation of basic techniques in the Newest Method of studying languages, the *Analytica* approaches its subject with an apparatus of definitions, axioms, and corollaries that mark it as a product of an age when Spinoza fashioned his *Ethics* into a geometric pattern and Hobbes found truth revealed in a proposition of Euclid. But the *Analytica* is not merely a new garb for the ideas of Comenius; it represents a significant change in his theory of method and at the same time reflects the growing rigidity of his thought, a growing tendency to systematize his lively notions into sterile inflexibility.[4] Comenius' search for a Baconian *filum labyrinthi* finally ended in a system of deductions based on suppositions canonized as axioms. The disciple of Bacon's and Campanella's anti-scholasticism, the admirer of Aristotle and the foe of Aristotelity, the tireless seeker for the thread of Ariadne heeded the consolations of pansophy and closed his intellectual life in the labyrinthine prison of his own *Novissima*.

Today it is easy enough to deride the theologico-scientific

3. In *VSJAK*, Vol. IV (1913), J. V. Novák makes a detailed comparison of the texts of the Czech and Latin didactics. A very significant discussion of the pedagogic and didactic endeavors of Comenius is to be found in the extensive introduction of Gustav A. Lindner to his German translation of the *Didactica magna* (Vienna and Leipzig, 1892). The most recent general analysis of the *Magna* is by D. O. Lordkipanidze, *Didaktika J. A. K.* (Tiflis, 1941), a work which I have been unable to examine.

4. Perhaps this view will have to be modified when all the texts of the recently discovered Halle manuscripts are made accessible. To date not one of the original Latin texts has been made available to the public. I have been able to examine only the Czech translations of the *Pampaedia* (1948) and the *Panorthosia* (1950). See Appendix III.

assumptions of pansophy[5] and to perceive that the vast but inadequate learning of the time doomed such ambitious attempts to failure; but in an age when Bacon took all knowledge for his province, when the parson Richard Burton preached medicine and the medic Thomas Browne diagnosed piety, the aspirations of the pansophists did not seem utterly chimerical even to shrewd politicians like Oxenstierna. Comenius was laboring in the great tradition of Vincent de Beauvais and preparing the way for Voltaire and Diderot, even though Bayle failed to appreciate Comenius' encyclopedic efforts.[6] Whatever the value of these efforts, it must be admitted that preoccupation with them had an unfortunate effect upon his didactic works. The genial, imaginative, and inventive qualities of his earlier works made not only for instruction but also for charm, whereas the later didactic works and the revisions of his earlier works are ensnared in the net of system and represent a less vigorous and less penetrating thinker. The philosopher-theologian gradually became the captive of his own single-minded program and lost the vision of discovery. The born psychologist and pedagogue fancied himself a pansophist, but his own age and succeeding ages have done him honor chiefly because of the original contributions of his younger days and because of the one later work which returned to those principles—the *Orbis pictus*.

The history of the germination, growth, and transformation of Comenius' ideas about method touches the intellec-

5. The term *pansophia* ("pansophy") is not original with Comenius; it seems to have been used first by Peter Laurenberg (1585–1639) in the title of his *Pansophia sive Paedia philosophica*.

6. In the *Dictionnaire historique et critique* (1695–97) Pierre Bayle dismisses Comenius' didactic work with this remark: "Ouvrage, dont la république des lettres n'a tiré aucun profit; et je ne pense pas qu'il y ait rien de practicable dans les idées de cet auteur."

tual history of the age at many points. From his earliest days as a theological student Comenius was interested in attempts to reform education, and in meditating on this subject he constantly strove to place his own theoretic concepts within the framework of a universal view, so as to be able to deduce consequences in all directions. With him a consideration of minor problems always led to an examination of large issues. As a young teacher in the Přerov Latin School, he attempted to facilitate the study of Latin by writing the *Grammaticae facilioris praecepta* (Praha, 1616), a book no longer extant but one which indicates by its title the bent of the young author's thoughts. He soon decided, however, that the question of making the study of Latin easier is only part of a larger problem—that of making all cultural studies more widely accessible and also more beneficial to all mankind. Even before the publication of this grammatical booklet he had begun, under the influence of his teacher, the encyclopedist Alsted, to collect materials for what we now know as the fragmentary *Theatrum universitatis rerum*. Originally he had intended this work as a guide to the Czech nation in the study of *realia*, but in a letter to Peter Montanus (1661) he describes the book as his *opus principale*, an encyclopedic work which will bear the title *Amphitheatrum universitatis rerum* and which will benefit all mankind by replacing a whole library of books.[7]

Thus in his early years as well as in his old age when he had become *praeceptor mundi*, Comenius took a large view of the task of education. He was not merely a reformer of method but also a pioneer in the attempt to educate a whole nation and later the whole world. In him the impulse toward

7. The work was to consist of twenty-eight books; the second book, containing a hundred and fifty chapters, perished in the Leszno fire, and the whole work was unknown except for title until a fragment of the manuscript was discovered in Holešov, Moravia, in 1893. Reprinted in *VSJAK*, Vol. I (5).

pansophy is humanitarian, even though his humanitarianism rests on notions of original sin and chiliasm. His is the titanic endeavor of a humble Christian to re-educate the heart of man, so that in the coming Golden Age the spirit would assert its domain over the body and order would triumph over chaos.[8] Whatever we may think of the wisdom of his pansophic schemes, this is the dominant and pervading idea in all his work—to benefit all humanity, whether the problem in hand be religious, scientific, or pedagogic. With all his patriotism and his complete devotion to the sect of which he was the last bishop, his final considerations are never nationalistic or sectarian but universal. It is also here that his closeness to Bacon is most striking. Whatever the similarities and differences between their methods and their opinions on particular aims and techniques, however far Comenius may depart from the experimental theories of Bacon, the animating purpose of both men is the same—to serve *Rex Humanitas*. To interpose the observation that Bacon was prone to identify the welfare of man with the welfare of the English imperium or that Comenius identified it with the glory of an Evangelical deity is merely to say that Bacon and Comenius were seventeenth-century Europeans, not Olympians.

This large hope of serving all mankind prompted Comenius to compose his first (Czech) didactic, which would be "useful not only for schools but for all humanity . . . not merely for the aristocracy of birth or intellect but for all men." In that work he also maintains, like Vives, that education should be made available to women, for he believes that a mother, being man's first teacher, should be well equipped for her task. The ninth chapter of the Czech

8. In the *Faber fortunae* and the *Centrum securitatis* Comenius describes man in his present state as the cruelest of animals. Chiliastic speculation was popular at Herborn when Comenius attended that university.

didactic contains one of his lesser-known but also one of his most engaging arguments on this point:

No reason can be shown why the female sex . . . should be kept from a knowledge of languages and wisdom. For they are also human beings, an image of God, as we are; they are also partakers of the mercy and the kingdom of the future life; in their minds they are equally gifted to acquire wisdom; indeed, in gentleness of understanding they are often more endowed than we. The Lord God likewise employs them sometimes in large affairs (to manage people, lands, estates, and even whole kingdoms; also to give special advice to kings and princes; also to practice the art of medicine and to care for fellow human beings; even to function as prophets and to aid priests and bishops in giving instruction and chastisement). Why then should we merely dismiss them with the ABC and drive them away from books? Are we afraid of their meddling? The more we introduce them to mental occupations, the less time they will find for meddling, which comes from emptiness of mind.

In his zeal to make every branch of knowledge available to all mankind, Comenius, although a child of the Reformation, cherished the medieval dream of harmonizing biblical revelation with all worldly science. At first he thought that this grand design could be wrought through the co-operative efforts of many scholars. Like the young Milton, he believed that a new Athens, a new republic of letters, could bring in a new age of general enlightenment. But finally after many disappointments he decided that he must undertake this superhuman task unaided. Thus the pansophic outlook found in his earlier works gradually develops into a far-reaching system that strives to embrace all knowledge. This system more and more dominates his didactic works and their subsidiaries, pedagogic aids like the revised *Vestibulum* and *Ianua*, for he intended to direct even his most elementary schoolbooks toward a common goal—an encyclopedic view of all existence.

The progressive difficulty of harmonizing various pedagogic works with his pansophic undertaking produced many labored and unfortunate changes in Comenius' conception and execution of his school texts. The difficulties of the problem were moral as well as intellectual. His own desire and the wishes of his learned friends, notably Hartlib, urged him toward the composition of encyclopedic works, but he was constantly being diverted from this task by the practical need of satisfying the Polish count Leszczyńsky and later the De Geer family in their demands for elementary textbooks, to say nothing of the demands made upon him as the spiritual head of his sect, the Unity of Brethren. This conflict of aims was most distressing to Comenius; his uncompromising honesty forced him to satisfy every obligation laid upon him, and his devotion to his ideals would not allow him to swerve from what he considered the highest function of his intellectual life. He resolved the difficulty by patiently though grudgingly elaborating new versions of his textbooks in an attempt to make them conform to his ever expanding views of pansophy.

Thus we see that the history of Comenius' pedagogic views is inherently a part of the history of his pansophic views and that the changing concepts of his didactics are determined by the ever growing scope of his "universal" program of education. Unfortunately no general estimate of his didactic and pansophic works, their range, tendency, and relative value, can be attempted before all seven of the newly discovered Halle manuscripts have been made accessible to public inspection.[9] Judging only from the Czech versions of the *Pampaedia* and the *Panorthosia*, one can discern in these long-lost works the growth of a grand system of all-embracing, all-penetrating definitions and deductions. This vast but incomplete intellectual drama is neither a prelude

9. See Appendix III.

to the damnation of Faustian arrogance nor a grand Miltonic argument to justify the ways of God; it is a humble though stupendous attempt to civilize the mind of man. Whatever its ultimate practical value, this heroic venture savors of magnificence.

The first pedagogic efforts of Comenius were prompted chiefly by a desire to aid his devastated homeland. At the very beginning of the Thirty Years' War the Battle of White Mountain (1620) had brought defeat and widespread misery to Bohemia. The intellectual leaders of the country went into exile or into hiding. For seven years Comenius remained in his native land, and, although he was a hunted man, he constantly sought and planned ways of deliverance from the calamities that had befallen his countrymen. Of all the remedies that offered, none seemed to him more promising than that of equipping young people with the best education possible, for, in his opinion, a well-educated generation would be the surest guaranty of a better future. Comenius therefore began to compose his educational works in Czech because he intended them solely for his countrymen.

At an early age he had begun to make collections for the *Theatrum* discussed above and also for a thesaurus of the Czech language, a work which perished in the Leszno conflagration. In 1627, while hiding from the agents of Emperor Ferdinand, he visited what had been the Zylvarov library in Vlčice and there came upon a German text of Elias Bodin's "natural" *Didactic* (1621). Taking a hint from the general plan of this work, he decided to write a systematic Czech didactic and also to provide his countrymen with a set of elementary but encyclopedic textbooks which would provide a well-planned approach to general culture. But in February, 1628, he was driven into exile, never to return. He sought refuge in the Polish town of Leszno, where some members of his sect had found asylum as early as 1548. During his first years in Leszno he looked upon his exile as merely temporary and therefore continued to work enthusiastically upon his Czech works, for he earnestly believed that, when Bohemia was liberated, his writings could aid in rebuilding the national culture which the Hapsburgs and the Jesuits endeavored to stamp out. Drawing upon his teaching experiences in Přerov, Fulnek, and Leszno, he set about the task of delineating a practical guide to general education. He also enlarged his outlook by extensive reading in the new literature of pedagogical realism, a movement which aimed to liberate schools from the purely one-sided discipline of linguistic and literary training and to extend the scope of education to the study of more practical matters—*realia*. The breadth of his explorations in the literature of educational philosophy is well attested by the contents of the *Methodus*.

Thus the project of Comenius grew in scope, and, in order to give a firm basis to the whole undertaking, he fashioned the Czech *Didaktika* into a broad statement of guiding cardinal principles. According to the program indicated in the *Didaktika*, he also intended to prepare a series of textbooks and various *informatoria* or guides for teachers. These works were to be used in the first three grades of his uniform school organization, that is, in the family, in the vernacular schools, and in the Latin schools. At this stage in his planning he did not consider the needs of the university, which was to be the fourth grade.

For the elaboration of this well-defined system of education based on definite principles the young author devised a comparative method which he prefers to call *syncritic*. His belief in the superiority of this method derives from his concept of revelation. Comenius thought that God had created all that exists in the universe and that he revealed himself and his work to mankind in three books: the book of nature, the book of the mind, and the book of Holy Writ. Since all three of these books have the same author, they are necessarily in complete and perfect agreement, and whatever is obscure in one book may become clarified by a parallel example in one of the other books. The parables of Christ are the chief exemplars of this sort of revelation and instruction; they are also the best evidence that this comparative method is the supreme method of teaching.

The modern reader may be left merely bored by Comenius' host of parables and parallels; he is certainly left unconvinced by this arbitrary and often fanciful method of exposition and proof, because fashions in thinking have changed and authority has shifted to other manipulations of fact and fancy. Many seventeenth-century readers, however, were receptive to this sort of argument and considered it with utmost seriousness. The strict logicians of course insisted on the old rule, "Similia nihil probant"; but Comenius, who termed his method "symbolic logic," countered with "Similia plus quam probant," for he believed that argument from similarity excels mere logical proof.

In the *E Scholasticis labyrinthis exitus* (*ODO*, Vol. IV), Comenius argues that no one understands a thing perfectly if he considers that thing in itself, whether analytically or synthetically; man acquires understanding of things only as he considers them in relation to other things. It is impossible to determine whether Comenius derived his syncritic method from Bacon's "inductive" method of comparison and contrast, or merely from the common rule, "Bene docet, qui bene distinguit," or from any one of a hundred other sources. This method has always held out a promise of revealing truth to those who assume an essential unity in the universe. It beckoned to analogists like Plato, universal historians like Orosius, and explorers of religious myth like Raleigh and

Selden. Nineteenth-century thinkers were still attracted to this procedure; note Comte's sociological comparisons, Taine's marriage of aesthetics and botany, and Spencer's whole system of analogical and comparative argument. The method fathered comparative philology and today dominates the search for an integration of knowledge. Comenius, like Frazer, sought for guidance in a golden bough.

Whatever the shortcomings of the Comenian method, the *Didaktika* is filled with suggestive analogies and vivid illustrations of idea; it also abounds in fruitful notions that have gradually revolutionized Western modes of instruction. Comenius urges us to banish despotism and terror from school discipline, to motivate learning through pleasure instead of fear,[10] to banish compulsion from all studies, to abolish the justification of *magister dixit* and give the reasons for professorial dicta, to supply short general outlines of a subject before plunging a student into a mass of details, to teach only what students can grasp, to provide carefully graduated instruction, to bring culture to the average mind and to the common man, to teach the mother-tongue, to educate the senses by opening the book of nature, to teach words in relation to things, and to require a student to engage in direct observation and individual practice lest his senses and mind become deadened by passive acquiescence to dogma. Comenius rejects the ascetic doctrine that man becomes virtuous by denying or suppressing his desires. The whole object of the *Didaktika* is to educate free men capable of entering into dignified relations with their fellows.

The pedagogic ideas of the *Didaktika* first achieved practical and concrete expression in the Czech versions of the

10. Most probably Comenius was unaware that two centuries before his time Vittorino Ramboldini da Feltre (1378–1446) had founded at Mantua a *casa giocosa* in which education was to be a delight instead of a wearisome task.

Informatorium and the *Ianua*. Although the *Informatorium
školy mateřské* ("Instructions of [for] the Mother-School")
remained in manuscript until 1858,[11] the work reached the
contemporary public through the German and Polish versions of 1633 and the Latin version of 1653.[12] The Czech
Ianua (*Dvéře jazyků otevřené* ["The Gate of Languages Unlocked"]), the only important pedagogical work of Comenius
published in Czech during his lifetime, was not printed until
1633 in Leszno, but a Latin translation of the work was
published in Leszno as early as 1631.[13] This Latin version,
entitled *Ianua linguarum reserata*, brought the author international fame; numerous translations of the work were
made into the chief European and even into some Asiatic
languages.[14]

Comenius, who had intended to address himself to the
Czech public and to reform Czech schools,[15] suddenly and

11. The *Informatorium* was begun perhaps as early as 1628 and completed about 1630. The manuscript, with Comenius' notes, is now in the
National Museum in Praha; it was discovered in Leszno in 1856 by Anton
Gindely and published by him (Praha, 1858). The Czech text was edited with
a commentary by J. Hendrich in 1925 and is also printed, together with
Comenius' own German translation, by J. V. Novák in *VSJAK*, Vol. IV
(1913). The Latin version appears in *ODO*, I, 197–249.

12. For an English version see W. S. Monroe, *The School of Infancy*
(Boston, 1896).

13. The *Ianua* was composed between 1629 and 1631; copies of the
original Czech and Latin editions are preserved in the municipal library of
Zittau in Saxony. The full Czech title reads: "The Gate of Languages Un-
locked, That Is, a Short and Easy Way of Understanding Any Language as
Well as the Beginnings of All the Liberal Arts, Wherein under a Hundred
Titles and in a Thousand Sentences All the Words of the Whole Language
Are Contained."

14. For the history of this work see Appendix II and also chap. viii of
the *Methodus*.

15. In 1632, during a temporary success of Protestant armies in Bohemia,
Comenius had high hopes of soon returning to his native land and of helping
to rebuild its schools; in that year he wrote *Navržení krátké o obnovení škol
v království českém* ("A Brief Proposal concerning the Renewal of Schools in
the Kingdom of Bohemia"), a work destined to remain in manuscript for

unexpectedly found himself famous in many foreign lands because of the Latin translation of his *Ianua*. This little book, which combined the teaching of languages with instruction in things, was a miniature encyclopedia of the sensible world. Whoever became acquainted with it in his native tongue and then studied the parallel Latin passages was well on the way of acquiring a knowledge of things as well as of Latin. The simple and practical method of this textbook appealed to teachers in many lands; hence the success of this unpretentious work, which during the seventeenth century remained the best known of Comenius' writings. Scholars and statesmen throughout Europe urged its author to devote himself to the reform of language-teaching,[16] and their entreaties, together with other reasons, finally diverted Comenius from his original purpose.

The political upheavals which had driven Comenius into exile made him a citizen of the world. His plans to write textbooks for Czech readers had to be modified, as is clearly indicated by the fate of the *Informatorium* and the *Ianua*. Although he never ceased to hope that Bohemia might regain its freedom and that he might return to help restore its culture, successive political disasters, notably the deaths of the "Winter King" of Bohemia[17] and of Gustavus Adolphus

almost three centuries. This work is now accessible in J. V. Novák's edition (Praha, 1925).

16. At various times during his life Comenius was asked to undertake the reform of schools in England, Holland, Germany, and Sweden; even from Catholic France he received an invitation by command of Cardinal Richelieu. The tradition that Comenius was asked to become president of Harvard College rests on an unconfirmed and seemingly erroneous statement in Cotton Mather's *Marginalia*, II, iv (see W. S. Monroe, *Comenius* [New York, 1900], pp. 78–81; Albert Matthews, "Comenius and Harvard College," *Publications of the Colonial Society of Massachusetts*, Vol. XXI [1919]; and Spinka, pp. 84–86).

17. Frederick, elector of the Palatinate, last king of an independent Bohemia; in 1613 he had married Elizabeth, daughter of James I of England; his daughter Sophia was the mother of George I of England.

in 1632, made it clear that his hopes would not be quickly realized. If Comenius was to obtain a hearing for his ideas, he would have to surmount the barrier of the vernacular and write in the language of the world. He therefore set about the task of composing his works in Latin and also of making Latin translations of his earlier writings.

The history of Comenian writings is a legend of irony.[18] The *Ianua*, which had been intended for a small nation, brought the author international fame. Comenius thereupon undertook to translate what he considered his most important work, the *Didaktika*, in order to acquaint the world with the fundamental principles upon which the *Ianua* was founded. He recast the *Didaktika* extensively, expanding certain parts and contracting others;[19] and by 1638, after years of labor, the new version was substantially complete. But the large international audience for which this magnum opus was intended turned out to be a small circle of friends who read the work in manuscript. In fact, the new version was not printed until nineteen years later, when it appeared, with some further changes,[20] as the *Didactica magna* in the first volume of the *ODO*.

Although the *Didactica magna* is today considered one of the great classics of pedagogy, it remained almost unknown for two hundred years. Its prolix and repetitious style, its lack of precise definition, and some of its rather trivial comments and illustrations displeased even sympathetic readers among the author's contemporaries, who could not perceive the bold and far-reaching reforms presaged in this work. In

18. The *Orbis pictus*, the most widely known work of Comenius today, was originally designed as an "auxiliary" text.

19. The differences between the Czech and Latin texts are analyzed by J. V. Novák in *VSJAK*, Vol. IV (1913).

20. E.g., in a letter (February 4, 1641) Comenius speaks of a *Posticum Latinitatis* which is to follow the atrial grade of study outlined in the *Didactica magna*, but the text printed in 1657 contains no such provision.

the eighteenth century the book was almost forgotten; indeed, it received no general recognition until the middle of the nineteenth century, when most of its principles had come to be accepted through the works of those who had borrowed their ideas from Comenius, either directly or indirectly.[21]

Comenius, inured to disappointment and defeat, was not disheartened by the unenthusiastic and even hostile reception given the *Didactic*. He answered fault-finding critics by showing that some of their objections were mere cavil; but, what is more important to the history of his works, he strove to elaborate his method, to extend its application,[22] and to give it a greater precision of statement. The *Ventilabrum sapientiae*,[23] in which he endeavored to reply to adverse criticism of his method, shows that Comenius was sharply aware of the faults imputed to him. A desire to correct some of these faults led him, when he was composing the *Methodus*, to construct a new didactic, the *Analytica*, in which he stated his method with less prolixity by striving for more precise definitions and more concise statement of principle.[24] Appendix I of the present work is designed to show how the kernel of the *Magna*, especially chapters xvi–xix, assumes new form in the *Analytica*.

The transition from the discursiveness of the *Magna* to the conciseness of the *Analytica* involves a far more complex and fundamental change than a superficial attempt to re-

21. A simple, brief, but very instructive survey of these borrowings is given by W. S. Monroe, *Comenius, the Evangelist of Modern Pedagogy* (Boston, 1892), pp. 142–72.

22. E.g., The *Dissertatio didactica* (1637), addressed to the authorities of the Breslau Gymnasium, is a detailed statement of how the principles of the *Didactic* can be applied to school organization.

23. Not published until 1657 in the *ODO*.

24. An even more concise analytical statement of the author's didactic principles is found in the posthumous *Consultatio catholica*, as printed by Nigrinus in the *Spicilegium didacticum* (Amsterdam, 1680).

duce verbiage. The change in style reflects a shift in the author's concept of what constitutes a didactic and what forms the basis of didactic principles. The *Analytica* is a true didactic, that is, a rationale of pedagogic method, whereas the longer Czech *Didaktika* and its Latin counterpart, the *Didactica magna*, are merely guides to methodical practice. Furthermore, the *Analytica* embodies a grand but perhaps unholy alliance between Comenius' theories of education and his pansophic and irenic dreams.

While working on the *Ianua linguarum*, Comenius had become so fully convinced of the practical value of pansophy that he decided to extend his reform in the teaching of languages to a reform in the teaching of *realia*. The direct result of this widened interest was the *Ianua rerum, sive sapientiae porta*,[25] a small encyclopedia of universal knowledge. This "Gate of Things" proposed to reveal the essentially uniform nature of all knowledge by proceeding, like the "Gate of Languages," in carefully graduated steps from the well known to the less well known. Each chapter would be a preparation for the next, and this cumulative process of learning would produce a unified body of knowledge. Unlike previous encyclopedias, the *Ianua rerum* would be arranged according to the learner's capacity. It would not be subdivided on the basis of a variety of subjects and therefore would not distract the learner by inconsistencies and contradictions; instead, by unifying all knowledge, it would resolve discords and create harmony of thought.[26] Thus pansophic endeavor, beginning with the most elementary kind of instruction, would develop into an irenic force not

25. Composed between 1640 and 1642 but not printed until 1681; a letter of 1642 indicates that Comenius had begun to make collections for a pansophic work as early as 1628.

26. It is easy to see why Comenius has been suspected of teaching pantheism and even of serving as a harbinger of Bergson and Croce.

only in religious controversy but in all other matters that touch the human understanding.

Comenius placed little faith in the ultimate value of contemporary scientific studies because he regarded them as unrelated and therefore incapable of ascertaining anything but fragments of truth. Since he considered incomplete and disconnected knowledge a source of confusion instead of certainty, he argued for the establishment of *one* science, all-science or pansophy, which would provide a dependable survey of all the knowledge derived from the three "books" of God. Knowledge based on such universal truths would lead to certitude and would command general acceptance; like mathematical demonstration, it would convince everyone with the force of self-evident truth. When we have achieved that kind of knowledge, we should be able to resolve all controversies by the harmonious evidence derived from an unvarying truth; such evidence leaves no room for doubt or contradiction. Once controversies are resolved by this irrefutable method, the results of controversies will be abolished, particularly the cruelest of these results—war. Then universal peace will rule throughout the world. Thus the pansophic ideal and the irenic hope coalesced in the dream of Comenius, and his chiliastic belief nourished the dream.

Like Plato and Bacon before him and like Shelley in later times, Comenius reshaped the universe in the image of his desire and ascribed reality to the fiction. As a poet he created visions of angelic understanding, but as a theologian and a schoolmaster he labored to codify his dream and thereby did violence both to science and to poetry. His once fertile imagination grew sterile at the touch of cold philosophy, and, when he recast his earlier inventions and discoveries, he misshaped them into a dogma at once pedestrian and visionary.

For all his self-scrutiny Comenius failed to perceive that his pansophy was but theology writ large and that even in this new guise the queen of the sciences forced her hand-maidens to manipulate evidence toward a favored end. The anagogical and teleological mode of his thought dulled his critical powers and betrayed him into arranging the problems of knowledge according to a formula that would yield predetermined conclusions. Thus he rejected the Copernican system because he could not reconcile it with his religious prejudices. Furthermore, like Hegel and Comte, he was bewitched by the magical properties of the triad and labored to harness phenomena and noumena into artificial trinities until his system became a host of troikas driving toward the land of Beulah.[27] It is no wonder that Descartes, although he approved the humanitarian impulse behind pansophic endeavors, dismissed the project of Comenius as pietism masquerading as science.[28]

The vision of a pansophic utopia captured the imagination of Comenius so completely that all his other works, except his religious writings in behalf of the Unity of Brethren, seemed to him of slight consequence. Dominated by a fixed idea, he recast the simple and readily teachable *Ianua* and *Vestibulum* into ontological and epistemological analyses of the chain of being. Thus even his practical and realistic notions about teaching became so vitiated by pansophy that they were transformed into a rigid system that deformed and maimed the author's ideas like the bed of Procrustes.

27. These trichotomies are reminiscent of the Paracelsan cosmic triad (salt, sulfur, and mercury); they may also be a reaction against the dualism of Campanella (cold and heat) and of Alsted (heaven and earth). Cf. Keatinge, I, 28.

28. A brief but useful discussion of Comenius' relations with Descartes and Mersenne is to be found in E. Čapek, *Komenský vychovatel* ("Comenius the Educator") (Praha, 1948), pp. 75–77.

During the years 1642–48 this builder of universal knowledge and universal peace was forced to relinquish his strictly pansophic works and devote himself to the lowly task of grinding out elementary textbooks for Swedish youngsters. Although punctilious in carrying out this distasteful task, he was determined not to compromise his ideals by abandoning what he considered his lifework. Resolving this difficulty in a characteristic way, he decided to elaborate an ultimate, definitive method which would give a philosophic basis to all education and would also serve as a blueprint for the required textbooks. It is for this reason that he composed the *Methodus novissima* and proceeded to reconstruct his textbooks according to this "latest" method. Hence the complete rewriting of the *Vestibulum* and the *Ianua*.[29] The Swedish authorities, notably Oxenstierna, who had only a slight interest in programs of universal knowledge but a keen interest in the immediate reformation of school curricula, constantly and impatiently urged Comenius to abandon his perfectionist schemes and to complete the promised textbooks. His son-in-law Figula aptly remarks in a letter of June 26, 1646: "It is his [Comenius'] weakness that he can never be satisfied with what he has done, and constantly hopes for greater perfection in everything." In a letter of June 15, 1647, Comenius himself confesses that his failure is the failure of Browning's Grammarian: "I could achieve more if I desired less."

Despite vexing difficulties Comenius persisted in his undertaking and after long delays completed his *Methodus* as well as the textbooks based on the analytical principles outlined in the tenth chapter of that master-work. This "new" method begins with complex wholes and ends with the minutest particles. The author explains in Section 62 of the *Analytica* that there exists hardly anything so simple that it

29. See Appendix II.

does not consist of parts, whether like or unlike. He therefore begins his exposition with a statement of the complex whole, "Didactics is the art of good teaching." But here spring up new "wholes": *teaching, good, art*. Therefore, Section 2 explains what is meant by *teaching, good teaching*, and *art of teaching*. As this analysis of successive concepts becomes more extended, the emerging subdivisions require further definition. Finally, we arrive at such "fundamental" notions as "We do not learn what we already know" (Axiom IV); "We learn the unknown only through the known" (Axiom V); and "We learn the unknown only by learning" (Axiom VI).

Such pronouncements are of little practical value, and an exposition of the principles underlying them is quite useless, since everyone accepts these ideas without benefit of detailed comment. It is true that the author's search for an exact and all-embracing method followed a mode of procedure common enough in his own time, but today, when empiricism is the fashion, that kind of thoroughness seems labored and pointless. Comenius also failed to perceive that, for all his insistence on reality and despite his rejection of verbalism, he was merely analyzing words and phrases to which he ascribed reality. He could not free himself from concepts of "absolute meaning" and "ultimate reality" because he never seems to have undertsood that definitions of words are merely descriptions of a small area of meaning. Consequently, his deductions end in statements of doubtful theoretical value and are not always inevitable conclusions to his premises. Thus the exact and methodical *Analytica* remains a mere shadow of the *Magna*.

At first glance the *Analytical Didactic*, because of its conciseness, coherence, and logical precision, appears superior to the *Didaktika* and the *Didactica magna*, but closer inspection shows how its rigorous systematizing is an unfortunate substitute for the fresh and original approach of the earlier works. This is also true of the new versions of the textbooks written to conform to the New Method. Scrupulously adhering to the principles of the *Analytical Didactic*, Comenius worked for several years on a revision of the original *Ianua* (1631) and *Vestibulum* (1633)[30] until he finally completed the task in 1648–49. But the new texts proved unwieldy and largely unusable. They have been consistently neglected by all but specialists, whereas the original texts long retained their vitality and were reprinted and imitated for generations.

Although the first *Ianua* had won immediate and widespread commendation throughout Europe, the author was dissatisfied with the work and repudiated the very principles upon which his famous book was constructed. Pursuing the logic of the *Analytica* to its inevitable conclusion, he devised a new *Ianua* in which he abandoned the simple parallelism of the earlier work. Because he wished to make this textbook an instrument of pansophic instruction, he enlarged its encyclopedic scope and replaced the lively descriptions of the original version by a presumably logical catalogue of phenomena. The result was a bulkier volume, richer in words and things but no longer a simple, practical introduction to language or to the everyday world under a child's observation.

This desire to systematize and synthesize all knowledge produced even more striking changes when Comenius revised his most elementary Latin textbook, the *Vestibulum*. While composing the first version, published in 1633, the author had been guided by the principle of "holding bricks together with lime." But in the late 1640's, when rewriting

30. Comenius wrote three versions of the *Vestibulum;* the significant changes in these texts are fully discussed by B. Ryba in "Komenského trojí zpracování Vestibula," *Archiv*, XV (1940), 29–41.

this primer according to the New Method, he rejected that earlier principle as the product of specious reasoning and insisted that "we must quarry stones one by one and shape them before we can attempt to use them for building." He was amazed at his own former lack of perspicacity and at his deluded attempt to begin the teaching of language by way of whole sentences, even the simplest. Accordingly, the new *Vestibulum* avoids the use of sentences but fails to achieve greater simplicity because it introduces a host of new concepts systematically classified.

According to the *Analytica*, the basic principles of the New Method require that the simple should lead to the complex, that the general should always precede the particular, and that all foundations must be ample enough to carry the weight of any structure to be erected upon them. The revised *Vestibulum* holds to these tenets with deadly earnestness. For the original sentence, "The smith hammers iron on the anvil," the analytical *Vestibulum* substitutes a catalogue of metals and an inventory of a smith's tools. Simple statements, such as "God is eternal, the world is temporal," are replaced by lists of isolated words arranged in supposedly logical categories: "All—something—nothing; god—world—man; thing—manner—motion; whole—part—absence of." In thus endeavoring to supply a broad foundation for his pansophic structure, Comenius merely succeeded in producing a pedagogic nightmare. He might just as well have undertaken to give elementary instruction in arithmetic by beginning with theories of number. He was writing schoolbooks but dreaming of universal wisdom and world peace.

From the distance of three centuries it is easy to detect the flaws in the evolution of Comenius' ideas. We can readily dissect and evaluate outmoded philosophies and antiquated intellectual conflicts, for we are left untouched by the social and political struggles that nourished those disputes of long ago. The havoc of wars in which we have had no part fails to obscure our vision or blunt our critical sense. Nor are we deluded by a seventeenth-century truce that promised to bring lasting peace to Europe. But Comenius, whose whole mature life was an experience of defeat, upheaval, and exile, shared the fond hopes of his time and sustained his courage by one passionate hope—the hope of ultimate peace. In Shelleyan manner he hoped till Hope created from its own wreck the thing it contemplated. He grasped at the best promises offered by the traditions to which he was born; to him Isaiah, Plato, St. Paul, Virgil, and Lucretius were true prophets, and with them he believed that "the old order changeth, yielding place to new." Assuming that life has a purpose and that that purpose is good, he persuaded himself that the destruction around him was not meaningless. God presumably destroys men who have been found unworthy and will replace them with those whose hearts and minds have been instructed in righteousness. Therefore, everyone who can help set the thoughts of men right should collaborate with God in bringing about this transformation.

The recently discovered Halle manuscripts show that Comenius was ready to make his contribution with a work of amazing scope: *De rerum humanarum emendatione consultatio catholica ad genus humanum, ante alios vero ad eruditos, religiosos, potentes Europae* ("General Consultation about the Improvement of Human Affairs [Addressed] to Humankind, above All to the Learned, Religious, and Powerful Men of Europe").[31] This is no Shavian survey of aeons but, in its author's opinion, a practical and immediate remedy for the ills of humanity. Comenius hoped that at the end of the Thirty Years' War the scholars, the clergy, and the statesmen of all Europe might be convoked in a grand synod

31. See Appendix III.

to formulate plans for a lasting peace. To this sage and learned assembly he intended to present his irenic scheme derived from pansophic thought, for he was convinced that, if peace is to endure, all men must be educated and instructed in a sure philosophy of living. He earnestly believed that his program of universal education, language, philosophy, and religion might serve as a basis for the deliberations of the creators of world-wide peace. Solomon's House and the Royal Society are narrow dreams beside the grandiose vision of Comenius. But, during the three centuries that the Royal Society has been enlightening the minds of men, the Latin originals of the Comenian design have not found a printer.

II

HISTORY OF THE *METHODUS*[1]

T HE remarkable success of his *Ianua linguarum* en-
couraged Comenius to undertake what he considered a
more significant work, the truly pansophic *Ianua rerum*.
Comenius announced this decision to his friend Samuel
Hartlib in London, to whom he sent a detailed report of the
project,[2] which Hartlib printed as *Conatuum Comenianorum
praeludia* (1637), republished later as *Pansophiae prodromus*
(1639). Attracted by Hartlib's promises, Comenius visited
England with the hope of organizing there a pansophic
academy.

While Comenius was in London conferring with the
pansophists and irenics in Hartlib's circle,[3] he received a
letter (October 9/19, 1641) from Ludovic de Geer, wealthy
French merchant living in Holland and procurer of military
supplies for Sweden. De Geer offered to aid Comenius' work
and invited him for a consultation. Unsettled political conditions in England and the rebellion of the Irish had turned
Comenius' lofty hopes of founding a pansophic college into

1. The genesis and development of the *Methodus* is recorded in the extensive though fragmentary remains of the author's correspondence in the
collections of Patera and Kvačala. The *Methodus* can be traced from its in-
ception to final publication in greater detail than any other work of Comenius. Much of the material in this section of the Introduction is derived
from Reber, pp. 185–93.

2. See G. H. Turnbull, *Samuel Hartlib* (London, 1920), p. 28.

3. Especially John Gauden, John Dury, Joachim Hübner, Theodore
Haak, and John Pell. For a richly documented study of the activities of this
group consult G. H. Turnbull's *Hartlib, Dury and Comenius* (London, 1947).

disappointment.[4] De Geer's offer, supported by the powerful Swedish royal chancellor Oxenstierna, promised definite employment in the preparation of textbooks for Swedish schools and, above all, an opportunity to serve the cause of Bohemia, for Comenius was convinced that Sweden would be grateful and would repay the services of Czech Protestants by throwing its great military power into the struggle for Czech independence. He therefore accepted De Geer's offer, despite the objections of his English friends, who considered the writing of textbooks of lesser importance than the building of pansophic academies. Comenius agreed with them but thought that he could combine work on textbooks with his pansophic endeavors.

But Oxenstierna, who was chiefly interested in the immediate problem of supplying texts for Swedish schools and who was eminently well informed about school systems and school organization,[5] insisted that the proper organization of schools must take precedence over pansophic and encyclopedic programs.[6] Finally, Comenius accepted the assigned task with reluctance. It is clear from the correspondence of this period that this work was substantially what later appeared as the *Methodus* and its attendant textbooks. In a letter dated November 18/28, 1642, he reported that he was settled in Elbing and that, although he was receiving some help from Paul Cyrill, Peter Figula, Daniel Peter, and Daniel Nigrin, he had only one real collaborator, George Vechner, who, however, intended to remain in Leszno. At the end of 1642 Comenius announced to Wolzogen, De

4. See R. F. Young (ed.), *Comenius in England* (London, 1932), and corrections by D. Stimson in "Comenius and the Invisible College," *Isis*, Vol. XXIII (1935).

5. For these negotiations between Comenius and Oxenstierna see especially Spinka, pp. 94–99.

6. He had examined the plans of Ratke and of Comenius and had judged Comenius' method superior.

Geer's manager, that he had spent a whole month in preparing for the assigned work and that during the coming year he would revise the *Ianua* and the *Vestibulum* in order to make them conform to the New Method and that he would add to these a *Ianua rerum*, which would contain the basis of all sciences and the foundations of pansophy.

The letters of the following year make it clear that the work was not progressing as rapidly as the author had hoped. Comenius' helpers proved of little use, and there were sectarian conflicts among his friends and allies and the perennial struggle within his mind whether to give precedence to pedagogic or pansophic undertakings.

In November, 1644, Comenius informed Gottfried Hotton, De Geer's friend in Amsterdam, that he would first complete his language textbooks but that he was also continuing his pansophic work. He repeatedly excused himself to De Geer for the delay in completing the assigned texts, but a letter of June 4/14, 1645, indicates that at that time his books on language must have been quite far advanced, for in this letter Comenius observed that a Stockholm printer should order paper in time for printing. Dr. Cyprian Kinner was now giving him valuable help as collaborator, and the work on the textbooks was progressing efficiently. But the fruitless religious negotiations at Orla, Lithuania, in August, 1644, and at Thorn in Poland, in August, 1645, which Comenius attended as a delegate for the Unity of Brethren, further delayed his work on the textbooks and brought stern reproof from the Swedish authorities. In September, 1645, De Geer threatened to dismiss Comenius for neglecting to fulfil his promises to the Swedes. Comenius renewed his efforts to complete the work, and on October 2/12, 1645, he informed Bishop Johannes Matthiae[7] that the

7. Famous Swedish theologian and bishop of Strengnäs, who had obtained for Comenius an audience with Queen Christina.

Methodus would be printed that winter; on the same day he sent to De Geer a detailed account of his work, saying that his task had been onerous because it involved both pansophic and pedagogic endeavors.

Finally, in 1646, the *Methodus* was completed but not printed. On January 5 of that year, Peter Figula, the son-in-law of Comenius, informed De Geer that the work would be on a grand scale but that it could not be published until all parts were brought into harmonious relationship. He also remarked that Dr. Kinner had undertaken to complete the textbooks while Comenius was devoting himself to the pansophic part of the work. In February, 1646, Comenius announced that arrangements were being made in Amsterdam for the publication of the school texts but that he could not submit any part of his work because the whole project had to be re-examined from its foundations. During June of this year, according to Figula, the works were being carefully revised, and, at last, on August 21, 1646, Comenius set out for Stockholm to present his works to a commission which, it is usually assumed, consisted of Chancellor Skytte and two Upsala professors, Loccenius and Freinsheim. The commission approved the works, but printing could not begin because the vast project called for a text, a grammar, and a lexicon for each of the three grades—vestibular, ianual, and atrial—that is, nine books altogether, exclusive of the *Methodus*. Cyprian Kinner was particularly helpful in composing the grammars and lexicons, the latter being largely founded on selections from the works of Gerhard Voss and Joseph Justus Scaliger and the *Thesaurus linguae Latinae* of Robert Étienne. That the whole laborious undertaking taxed the patience of Comenius is evident from his letter to Hartlib (December 27, 1646), which is bitter and even complains of lack of generosity on the part of De Geer.

Finally, part of the *Methodus* was sent to Sweden in

December, 1646; the remainder was dispatched in February, 1647, together with part of the new *Ianua*. In May, 1647, Comenius promised the *Vestibulum* and in June the rest of the *Ianua*. The first printing was to consist of five hundred exemplars to be submitted to the judgment of the learned in order to benefit from their criticism in the further preparation of the work.

Why the printing in Sweden was put off is not quite clear. Perhaps Bishop Matthiae's lack of enthusiasm for the New Method was the cause; he is said to have considered the *Methodus* merely another wordy phrasing of general ideas. Or perhaps the practical parts of the work (especially the *Atrium*) were still incomplete.

In the summer of 1647 Comenius was still occupied with correcting the *Methodus*. The task was so exacting that, as he writes to Ritschel, one of his collaborators, he could not devote himself to anything else; furthermore, he wished to let Dury look over the work in order to benefit from the criticisms of that famous irenic.

At the beginning of 1648 Comenius was working alone, for even his last helpers had left him. The introductory *Methodus* was not in print, and the school texts had not been completed, notably the third part, the *Atrium*, with its grammar and lexicon. Under these conditions Comenius returned with his works to Leszno at the end of July, 1648, having been elected bishop of his sect. Finally, in Leszno the work was put into print, but even now there were delays. Only a small number of copies was ordered, whether five hundred or only two hundred is not clear,[8] these first printings being intended only as specimens for criticism.

By September, 1648, only 192 pages had been printed, whereas the completed work contains 608 pages, exclusive of introduction and index. It is therefore clear that the whole

8. Cf. Reber, p. 188.

work, with its 37-page index, could not have been printed in full until the following year (1649). Because of difficulties with printers, Comenius did not undertake to publish the textbooks, intending to send them to Amsterdam, where they would be well edited without expense to the author. At best the income from these books would be small because many scholars were asking for free copies.

From the evidence extracted from the correspondence it is possible to assign 1649 as the date of the Leszno edition of the *Methodus*, although 1648 is the date mentioned in a letter to P. Montanus. As for the Latin textbooks, it appears that they were composed by 1648 but not ready for print. The new *Vestibulum* and *Ianua* may have been completed but were not printed in that year; the *Atrium* did not appear until 1652.

The sources and aids for the composition of the *Methodus* are fairly well indicated in chapter viii, where Comenius lists twenty-five scholars whose works he had utilized; throughout the whole book he discusses more than forty great Renaissance scholars to whose works he was indebted for various suggestions—an indebtedness which he usually indicates with scrupulous honesty. In the present work the footnotes to the summaries of the various chapters attempt to indicate the nature and the extent of that indebtedness. Comenius' chief collaborators in his large undertaking were at first Johannes Rave and George Ritschel, later Dr. Johannes Sofronius Kozák, and, finally, Dr. Cyprian Kinner, who seems to have been his most dependable helper in revising the *Vestibulum* and the *Ianua* and in writing the *Atrium*, a new work.[9]

The *Methodus* immediately won high commendation from enthusiasts. Among the first to acclaim it were Peter

9. The revised *Vestibulum* and *Ianua* were completed in 1649; the *Atrium* appeared in 1652. See Appendix II.

Colbovius of Gadebusch in Mecklenburg; Adam Weiheimer, superintendent of schools in Esslingen; and Count Opaliński, who introduced the New Method in Sirakov. But Comenius himself thought that the praise accorded his work was excessive and that the book was full of faults (*ODO*, IV, 5–8). He realized that many parts should be altered but felt that he was too old to undertake extensive revisions of this large volume (*ODO*, IV, 48–54). The tenth chapter (the *Analytical Didactic*) he considered sound but too wordy; nor was he satisfied with the title *Novissima*, for he realized that there would be other attempts to improve methods of teaching languages and that these new methods would certainly be refinements on his work.

III

CONTENTS OF THE *METHODUS*

1. The TITLE-PAGE of the first (Leszno, 1649?) edition of
the *Linguarum methodus novissima*[1] announces that the
"New Method of Languages is firmly constructed on didactic foundations, specifically demonstrated by example of the
Latin tongue, adapted with utmost precision to the use of
schools, but also adaptable, with great profit, to other kinds
of studies." The work is "submitted to the public judgment
of learned and exacting critics." A text figure carries the
favorite motto of Comenius: "Let violence be absent. Let all
things flow spontaneously." The title-page carries neither
imprint nor date.

LINGUARUM

M E T H O D U S

NOVISSIMA,

FUNDAMENTIS DIDACTICIS SOLIDÈ SUPERSTRUCTA:

LATINAE LINGUAE EXEMPLO REALITER DEMONSTRATA:

SCHOLARUM USIBUS JAM TANDEM EXAMUSSIM AC-

COMMODATA:

SED & IN SUPER ALIIS STUDIORUM GENERIBUS MAGNO

USU ACCOMMODANDA.

ANTE TAMEN

ERUDITORUM JUDICIO PUBLICE EXPOSITA, SERIJSQ(UE)

AC SEVERIS CENSURIS SUBMISSA.

ABSIT VIOLENTIA REBUS. OMNIA SPONTE FLUANT:

À

JOHANNE COMENIO

MORAVO.

1. The second (Amsterdam, 1657) edition bears the title *Novissima
linguarum methodus*.

2. GREETINGS to the printers, "men of light"; a warning against the printing of unauthorized texts. [Not in the second edition.]

3. DEDICATION to Master Ludovic de Geer, whose generosity and forbearance have enabled the author to devote six years to this "philological lucubration." Comenius begs forgiveness for the long delay in publication; he includes praise for the sons of De Geer and manages to introduce a wealth of learned quotations and references: Plato, Horace, Dionysius of Halicarnassus, Isocrates, Virgil, Martial, Aristotle, and modern scholars like Robert Étienne, Eilhard Lubin, and John Sturm. Biblical echoes and references also abound, these being intended to please the taste of De Geer, a serious-minded adherent of church reform. Flattering references to the ancient and honorable ancestry of De Geer are joined to a biblical "Lausque Tua non ex hominibus, sed ex Deo est" (Rom. 2:29). The dedication is "given" at Elbing[2] in East Prussia, "toward the close of the year 1648."

4. TABLE OF CONTENTS: the headings of the thirty chapters of the book arranged as an outline of the whole work.

5. PREFACE, addressed to "truly erudite men." Animadversions on the sad state of human affairs in Europe. The author discusses his beloved trichotomy[3] and shows how it manifests itself in all human undertakings and how it mirrors the nature of the triune God. In his lament over the sufferings caused by the Thirty Years' War (Sec. 8), he bewails violent political factions and the unbridled zeal of theologians ("tam violentus est politicarum rationum status ille concursus et tam atrox tamque malum exasperans

2. Then under the protection of the Polish king; a city of particular interest to students of English history because from 1560 to 1626 it was the seat of the English Eastland Company and the sole trading center for English goods in the Baltic.

3. As exemplified in human affairs by the triad of learning, government, and religion.

theologorum infrenatus zelus") until he is forced to admit the justness of the atheist's comment: "To so much evil has religion been able to persuade mankind" ("Tantum religio potuit suadere malorum").[4] School, government, and church, which ought to show the way to human happiness, have been the chief centers of controversy. As a result learning has suffered, but scholars, like farmers, can repair damage through industry. The author himself has made his contribution by trying to reform the study of language. His earlier works, although favorably received by the public, did not satisfy him; therefore, he tried to improve them and make them more useful for teachers and students by devising a new method based on three guiding principles: (1) exact parallelism between things and words; (2) gradual and unbroken progression; and (3) uniform arrangement that would insure a fruitful and easy use of this method, in which practice by the student is imperative.[5]

One cannot construct a method for the study of languages without inquiring into the precise nature of language; therefore, the present work will first discuss the origin, nature, and development of language in general (chaps. i–vi). It will then consider the special difficulties in the study of Latin under former methods (chaps. vii–ix) and the means of making that study pleasant and rapid (chaps. x–xvii).[6] Finally, it will show how the New Method can benefit youth, schools, and all other human undertakings (chaps. xviii–xxx). The author is concerned not merely with the study of Latin but with the study of all languages, not merely with

4. Lucretius *De rerum natura* i. 101.

5. The special virtues of the New Method are discussed in chap. viii, which is an outline of pedagogical history in the sixteenth and seventeenth centuries, from Melanchthon to the contemporaries of Comenius.

6. These eight chapters outline the New Method; thus the actual delineation of Comenius' method occupies only about one-third of the whole work.

the cultivation of language but with the cultivation of the soul. The author calls special attention to chapter x and its detailed exposition of the technique of teaching. He scorns superficiality and distrusts structures built without proper foundations. Since he has always proposed to himself universal ends, he must seek sure and solid means to attain those ends. That is the reason for the prolixity of his work; like Horace, he will labor to be brief, not obscure.[7]

6. THE BODY OF THE WORK. As noted under No. 4 above, Comenius gives a skeleton outline of the thirty chapters of the *Methodus*. In the following paragraphs I have attempted a brief summary of those chapters in order to place the *Analytical Didactic* within its context.[8]

Chapter i.—Reason, language, and freedom of action are special gifts which God bestowed upon man and thereby elevated him above the brutes; thus philosophy, philology, and philotechny originate with Adam. As Cardan (*De subtilitate* xi) rightly asserts, reason, language, and the hand are the implements of divine wisdom. Reason gives us understanding of things; language enables us to report things; the hand, to perform them. The cultivation of these endowments has been left to human industry and ingenuity. Those who neglect these gifts will be stupid, inarticulate, and slothful; they will be merely shadows of men, not far removed from brutish ignorance. The eye is a divine gift, but observation is the task of man; the tongue is an instrument of God, but language is the creation of man; the hand is the workshop of God, but the achievements of the hand are the glory of man. All these gifts must be cultivated from infancy. To speak or to act without understanding is

7. Cf. *Epistles* ii. iii. 25, 26.

8. For a more detailed analysis see Ernst Liese, *Des J. A. Comenius Methodus linguarum novissima: Inhalt und Würdigung* (Bonn, 1904); Novák (Novák-Hendrich, pp. 394–405) gives a brief but instructive summary of each chapter.

senseless. Speech is merely a special kind of action; both speech and action must be brought under the control of reason. Therefore, no discussion of language can neglect reason and action.

Chapter ii.—The nature and the uses of language. Adopting the notions of the founder of the Stoic school, Chrysippus,[9] perhaps by way of Varro,[10] Comenius insists that the mind is the source of speech; he readily accepts the mentalist and analogist views which had bedeviled European philology since Plato's *Cratylus*.[11] As he restates and develops his cherished notion that words and things are related and therefore should be studied together, he asserts that language consists of three ingredients: (1) things indicated; (2) thoughts communicated; and (3) words articulated. Language is like a painting; the speaker presents pictures of things to the hearer, for speech is the expression of thoughts, and thoughts are the images of things. Thus language is concerned with things, perception of things, and verbal expression of things. Consequently, an author should take pains (1) to write about things that are true and good; (2) to use appropriate words in order to make himself understood; and (3) to observe the rules of language. The apparatus of a perfect language consists of (1) a full nomenclature, that is, a word for each thing; (2) an exact terminology, that is, full agreement on the meanings of words; and (3) a full set of laws for regulating the language, that is, dependable rules of syntax. Therefore, every language should possess, besides a complete vocabulary, accurate dictionaries and grammars.[12]

9. *Perì tês anōmalías, Perì etymologikôn, Perì tôn toû lógou merôn.*— Reber, p. 221.

10. *De lingua Latina* vi. ii.

11. Comenius also shared with Bacon and Hobbes the seventeenth-century interest in what is nowadays popularly known as semantics.

12. Throughout his life Comenius endeavored to secure or to produce satisfactory lexicons.

Existing languages are at fault in that they lack words for
certain things and assign several meanings to a single
word.[13]

Language is of three kinds: (1) gesture or silent language,
which is the necessary language of deaf-mutes and an
auxiliary to speech; (2) spoken language; and (3) written
language, which is the crown of language because it fixes
expression. Writing can represent ideas, pictures, or sounds;
this last kind of writing is the most perfect. Here Comenius
follows Bacon in commenting on the value of Chinese "mental characters . . . which men of different languages can use
for communication"; these characters Bacon had called
"real, not nominal," because they "express not letters and
words, but things and notions."[14] But, like Bacon, Comenius
concludes that our mode of writing is superior because of its
facility, speed, and "perfection." He also recommends
tachygraphy as one of the perfect forms of writing because it
multiplies books with astonishing speed.[15]

Chapter iii.—The variety of languages in the world.
Adam spoke one language, but his descendants employ
different words for the same thing; for example, *kephalē,
caput, haupt, head, glowa, hlava.* These variations on one
original speech result from the confusion of tongues during
the building of the Tower of Babel; thus God's edict is the

13. At this point Comenius discusses homonyms, synonyms, and *polysema*
("words of many meanings"); his comments are quaintly amusing, especially when he records Greek *hêpar* ("liver") and *splēn* ("spleen") as Latin
and calls German *Ross* and *Pferd* "idle synonyms" (*otiosa synonyma*).

14. *De dignitate et augmentis scientarum*, VI, i. par. 3.

15. Comenius was keenly interested in shorthand; in 1641, writing from
England, he reported that this new art of writing had spread even to English
villages. Reber (p. 229), to whom I owe this reference, is at fault when he
assigns the invention of modern shorthand to the time of James I. After the
Tironian system fell into disuse, stenography was reborn in England with
the publication of Timothy Bright's *Characterie* (1588) and John Willis'
Arte of Stenographie (1602).

first reason for linguistic diversity. Other reasons are human volubility and the mixture of races. Furthermore, a language may undergo internal changes; Plato (*Cratylus* xxxiii) and Polybius (*Histories* iii) bear witness that Greek and Latin had undergone profound modification in ancient times. Subsequently Latin degenerated into Italian, and similar changes took place in Germanic and Slavic. The number of languages in the world is uncountable, because no one can tell how many of them, like nations, have perished (e.g., Old Prussian). In modern Europe there are four linguistic branches: Latin has diffused itself into Italian, Spanish, and French; Mother German has produced Dutch, Danish, Swedish, English, Icelandic, and perhaps some others; and Slavic has given rise to Croatian, Bohemian, Serbian, Polish, Ruthenian, Muscovite (Great Russian), and Bulgarian. Hungarian cannot be related to any of these but is cognate with the languages of Asia, whence it came.

At some future date the author hopes to prove, by means of a synoptic lexicon (*lexico . . . harmonico*),[16] the identity of the four European groups of languages, their connection with Hebrew, and the primacy of Hebrew.[17] The original language was the language of the patriarchs. The differences among present-day languages prove the unnaturalness of all extant speech, for whatever is natural is common to all men, as, for instance, the body and its organs of sense. We still may hope to construct a language somewhat like the original natural language, at least in the sound of its words, their formation, and their meanings. Exemplars of this sort of

16. Note the author's constant preoccupation with pansophic and encyclopedic schemes; the production of practical textbooks was to Comenius an enforced and distasteful interruption of what he considered his great task, that of enriching mankind with knowledge of universal scope.

17. Like most of his contemporaries, Comenius believed in the monogenetic theory of language and in the notion that Hebrew was the ancestor of all other languages.

speech can be found in interjections and onomatopoetic words.

Chapter iv.—The comparative study of language is filled with great difficulties because the dissimilarities among languages appear to outnumber the similarities. All languages express things by means of words but employ different methods of expression. Every language, whether Spanish, Bohemian, Arabic, Mongolian, or Inca, has its special claim to excellence and also its particular shortcomings.[18] Some languages have fewer words than there are things; hence they represent several things by one word. Others have more words than there are things; these use several words to express the same thing. Furthermore, the number of letters in each alphabet is different: 23 in Latin, 24 in Greek, 28 in Arabic, 32 in Dalmatian,[19] 33 in Armenian, 47 in Abyssinian. Languages also differ in general structure; Chinese, for instance, is monosyllabic, whereas Hungarian is highly polysyllabic. These differences extend to sounds, syllables, genders, numbers, cases, declensions, and conjugations.[20] Besides, each language has its special idioms and

18. Perhaps because he was literally a citizen of the world, Comenius, although devoted to his native speech, could always take this detached view of national claims to greatness. He spent almost the whole of his mature life in exile, laboring and sacrificing himself for the welfare of his countrymen. At the age of seventy-six he wrote, "My life here was not my native land, but a pilgrimage; my home was always changing, and nowhere did I find a resting place" (*Unum necessarium* [Amsterdam, 1668]).

19. A Romance language, said to have become extinct with the death of Antonio Udina in 1898.

20. Comenius commends Bohemian because it avoids useless letters and praises English because it dispenses with gender in designating inanimate objects (Sec. 14). His generalizations are based merely on certain groups of languages; hence his assertion that all languages inflect nouns and verbs (Sec. 13) and that all have three persons (Sec. 16). On the basis of verbal endings he asserts that Greek, Bohemian, Latin, and German must be cognate (Sec. 18).

dialects, and all these differences are constantly being multiplied as languages continue to develop.

The author cannot subscribe to Bacon's opinion that highly inflected languages are necessarily more expressive and more useful than those of simpler structure.[21] A language rich in forms is difficult to learn; wealth of inflection is an impediment to the learning of things.

Linguistic unity is prevented by the human struggle for precedence. Nations contend with one another because of exaggerated vanity and universal jealousy. A boastful conviction of one's own superiority and an absurd contempt for whatever is foreign create major obstacles to common understanding. Certainly no modern language can make high pretensions to superiority, for a language achieves excellence only through centuries of cultivating graceful expression and apt usage. No modern tongue has had a sufficiently long tradition to acquire the polish of the classics. That is why the most valuable languages to study are those ancient tongues which contain the treasures of divine and human wisdom: namely, Hebrew, the sacred or prophetic language; Greek, the sapient or apostolic language; and Latin, the erudite or ecclesiastical language.[22] Even a cursory examination reveals how large a debt every modern language owes to these ancient tongues. Therefore, instead of fomenting a

21. Cf. Bacon's *De augmentis*, VI, i, par. 6. In his note on this passage, James Spedding suggests that Bacon was "probably the first to propose" this question. Spedding also calls attention to Grimm's refutation of the opinion that complex morphology makes for subtlety of expression: the thirteen cases of the Finnish noun should make Finnish much subtler than classical Greek, with only five cases (*Transactions of the Berlin Academy*, 1852). Comenius' argument, earlier than Grimm's by two hundred years, is based, characteristically, on grounds of utility.

22. The first is the language of the Old Testament, the second of the New Testament, and the third of the Church Fathers. These three, as Reber notes (p. 249), Luther had called "the sheathes in which the word of God is thrust like a knife" ("Scheiden, darin dies Messer des Geistes, Gottes Wort, steckt").

senseless competition among our languages, we should devote ourselves to an earnest and zealous cultivation of every
language. But nationalist pride makes every speaker glorify
his own tongue, and nations try to outshine, overcome,
oppress, and finally destroy one another. Would that they
strove to outdo one another in culture!

Chapter v.—No language has reached perfection because
no nation has fulfilled its obligations to its own language.
Men have neglected to make full and proper use of the triple
instrument for the cultivating of language: (1) nomenclature, that is, a systematic way of naming things; (2) lexicons
of words and phrases; and (3) grammars. The naming of
things is the very basis of all language, but men have failed
to make words conform to things, to human reason, and to
one another. Pliny, Hesychius, Suidas, and Julius Pollux
have supplied us with rich treasuries of words, but their
lexicons are not simple enough for ordinary use, nor are they
really practical, because their definitions are not sufficiently
precise. Greek, Latin, and Hebrew philologians have produced scholarly grammars, but these works, by their very
nature, fall short of the ideal practical grammar, which
should be complete, accurate, easy, and pleasing. Because of
this lack of proper lexical and grammatical equipment, the
study of languages, instead of making progress, has thus far
led only to inefficiency and dissatisfaction. Hence we are
justified in trying to bring about a reform in methods of
language study, so that every language may be cultivated
more fully than hitherto. Of course all languages cannot be
cultivated to the same degree, for, when nations are un-
acquainted with certain objects, they also lack names for
those objects; indeed, no extant language has been developed to its full potentiality.

Chapter vi.—Wisdom does not depend on the knowledge
of many languages; indeed, it would be a happy state if we

had only one language, so that we could concentrate on the study of things instead of words. Of course it is necessary to know several languages if we are to engage in comparative studies and strive for universal education; our relations with various nations also require that we know many languages. But, in order to improve the study of all languages, it is necessary to cultivate one of them especially. Everyone should devote himself to a careful study of one language because (1) the more a language is cultivated, the more it will grow to perfection; (2) the more perfect a language, the more it can contribute to the refining of other languages; and (3) the more a language is used, the more readily can it become a world language and a bond among nations.

Some languages achieve primacy because they are richly developed (Greek), others are spread through religious zeal (Arabic through Mohammedanism), but most commonly a language is diffused by the growth of empire (Latin and Quechan, the language of the Incas).

Among the many "universal" languages of the world, Latin is best fitted for use as a general language of instruction because from ancient times it has served as a means of communication among nations. As Vives has aptly stated,[23] Latin is pre-eminently the language of general education because it is a repository of universal learning and a treasury of wisdom, so that it has had a far-reaching effect on the spiritual development of mankind. Furthermore, it is a rich and polished idiom which serves as an excellent introduction to the study of other languages; indeed, knowledge of Latin is a firm basis for the mastering of other languages. Latin is also comparatively easy to learn; herein it is superior to

23. Here Comenius quotes a long passage from Vives and refers to the third book of *De tradendis disciplinis*, which is the tenth book of *De disciplinis* (Bruges, 1531). For more detailed information see the *Analytical Didactic*, Sec. 98, n. 18, p. 153, below.

Greek, which it "leaves many parasangs behind" in the matter of facility and regularity. Greek presents labyrinthine difficulties, but Latin is difficult to learn only because it is taught by wearisome, involved, and harsh methods. It is true, as Lubinus observes,[24] that through their lowly tasks camp followers and menials learn two or three languages radically different from their own in less time than our students learn Latin through concentrated and laborious study. But, since Latin is comparatively simple in pronunciation, definite in meaning, and regular in structure, the difficulty of learning the language must be ascribed to the inadequate and faulty methods of our instruction.

Chapter vii.—Wherein are current methods at fault? How can we devise a better method, one which could be also used for the teaching of other languages? The ancients learned Latin through daily conversation, but this "direct" method is imperfect because it takes too much time and gives one only a fragmentary and superficial knowledge of a language. Furthermore, in our day Latin is largely confined to books, and books are mute conversationalists; they cannot clarify meaning by means of gesture or rephrasing. Therefore, we must depend upon systematic methods and the artificial aids of terminology, dictionaries, and grammars. But the customary methods, as Lubinus has shown,[25] seem to have been invented for the express purpose of wasting time and preventing a student from learning Latin. Apparently an

24. Eilhard Lubin of Amerland (1565–1621), professor of mathematics and theology at Rostock; known for his polemical writings on theology, his editions of Greek poets, and a variety of books on language (*Antiquarius, Trinae satyricorum paraphrases, Clavis Graecae linguae*). The present citation is from what Comenius designates as Lubin's "Didactic," which is not an independent work but merely a twenty-four page prefatory epistle to the second edition (1617) of Lubin's trilingual (Greek-Latin-German) New Testament, first published in 1614. Comenius held this "Didactic" in high regard and cities it repeatedly throughout the *Methodus*.

25. See n. 24.

evil spirit, aided by ill-omened monks, introduced these methods into our schools so that with great labor we could achieve an abortion of Latin, defiled by Germanisms, solecisms, and barbarisms.

There are three major faults in current methods. In the first place, Latin is taught abstractly; that is, words are equated with words. Our pupils are taught to translate the vernacular into Latin without understanding the meaning of the vernacular words. Thus they merely substitute meaningless vocables for others equally meaningless.

The second fault is that we perplex beginners with the intricacies of formal grammar and require them to analyze linguistic structure before they have any knowledge of linguistic matter. This would not be a grave error if they knew something about the structure of the vernacular, but no one has yet proposed that schools teach the vernacular as formal grammar. The result is that pupils consider grammatical structure a peculiarity of Latin. What is worse, the grammars which they study are not written in a language they understand but in Latin, the very language that they are trying to learn. Would an adult attempt to learn Arabic or Mongolian with the aid of grammars written in those languages? Yet, when we deal with young pupils, we follow the absurd practice of forcing them to struggle simultaneously with the words of a rule, with the meaning of the rule, and with the genius of an alien speech. We need not comment on the effect produced by the multitude and the obscurity of these stupefying rules.

The third fault of existing methods consists in their lack of graduated exercises. We force our pupils to make impossible leaps; we expect them to undertake the study of grammar by beginning with the epistles of Cicero and the eclogues of Virgil; we ask them to walk on air, to fly before they have wings. The epistles are addressed to mature minds, and the eclogues present enigmas even to the teacher. These writings deal with an antiquity that is largely unknown to us; therefore, they require careful historical scrutiny before they can be comprehended. Besides, their lofty and elaborate style is wasted on stammering youth. If Cicero visited our schools and saw how children are tormented with his texts, he would be moved to laughter or to indignation. In the *De oratore* he himself protests against the teaching of oratory to those who have not mastered speech.

Some teachers defend current practice by arguing that they merely intend to acquaint pupils with words and phrases. But it is a grievous mistake to divorce words from meanings; such training is fit only for parrots. Why give a pupil a scabbard without a sword? Why build a tower from the top down? Still others maintain that current methods set up a perfect model toward which pupils may strive. But such aspiration has no point unless it offers hope of achievement; stammering youngsters cannot suddenly attain lofty eloquence. All training should progress gradually; growing maturity will supply the occasions and the ability to advance in learning. Neither nature nor art proceeds by leaps; work of lasting value must advance step by step. If our approach to such writers as Cicero, Terence, Virgil, and Ovid is to be profitable, it must be gradual. The observations of the great master Vossius[26] bear witness how the minds of the young are dulled by masses of rules and exceptions, particularly since many of those rules are false.

26. Johannes Gerhard Voss of Heidelberg (1577–1649), professor at Leyden and Amsterdam; theologian, philologian, and polyhistor; in his own day considered the foremost authority on Roman literature. The reference here is to *De arte grammatica* (Amsterdam, 1635), Book vii, chap. i. "This work was long considered unsurpassable."—Reber.

Chapter viii.[27]—The inadequacy and faultiness of current methods have long been recognized, and many attempts have been made to bring about a reform. But these attempts have usually been too restricted in scope to effect the radical improvement which is needed.

Among those who have tried to remedy existing confusion, the chief controversy has centered in the question whether Latin should be taught by precept or by use. The two schools of thought are well represented by Melanchthon, the restorer of letters in Germany, and by the renowned Lubinus. Melanchthon[28] insists on the teaching of formal grammar and inveighs against those who would teach Latin by use alone. He believes that such ill-advised practice results in unsound instruction and exercises a harmful effect upon the whole life of a student and the society in which he lives. Contempt for the rules of grammar breeds contempt for the rules of other arts and engenders a lack of respect for the rules that govern private and public morals.

Lubinus,[29] on the other hand, considers the teaching of formal grammar an impediment to learning, a needless torture, and a represser of talent. He recommends, instead, the daily practice of conversation in Latin as the most efficient way of acquiring the language. Although his plan is unac-

27. This chapter forms a historical sketch of theories and practices in language-teaching from the early sixteenth century through the first half of the seventeenth.

28. Philip Melanchthon (Schwarzert) (1497–1560), the famous leader of the Reformation and author of the Augsburg Confession, was also renowned as a philologian and a reformer of German letters; educated at Tübingen; professor of Greek and of theology at Wittenberg; translated Hesiod into Latin. Comenius makes use here of various passages from the Preface to Melanchthon's *Syntaxis* (Nuremberg, 1565).

29. For Lubinus see n. 24 above. In the present chapter Comenius rejects this proposal of teaching Latin solely through conversation, but in a later work (*Latium redivivum*, 1657) he recommends the learning of Latin "by use alone."

ceptable, he does make the highly practical suggestion that
language be studied through books in which short sentences
employing all the words and phrases in a language are
illustrated by pictures of the things discussed.[30]

The opponents of formal grammatical instruction are
many. Even the great Lipsius[31] regrets the years he wasted
on grammatical trifles when he could have been acquiring
solid knowledge. Caselius recommends the early reading of
Latin authors and constant practice in composition; he
makes the impractical suggestion that youngsters learn
Latin by reading the classics and by using them as material
for elementary exercises.[32] Frey agrees with Lubinus in that
he advocates the founding of colleges in which Greek and
Latin would be spoken during all daily activities, so that
students would be constantly exposed to choice classical
diction. He believes that within five years they would thus
acquire a finer command of Roman Latin and Attic Greek
than do those who spend ten years in classroom study of
these languages.[33] Although the value of this conversational
method is attested by the experience of Montaigne,[34] such a
procedure would be of little benefit to the general public if

30. A forecast of Comenius' own *Orbis pictus* (Nuremberg, 1658).

31. Justus Lipsius (Joest Lips) (1547–1606), professor of history at
Louvain; learned editor of Seneca and Tacitus. The reference here is to No.
94 (November 11, 1582) of his *Miscellaneous Epistles*. Cf. Reber, p. 284.

32. Johannes Caselius (1533–1613), professor of rhetoric and of philosophy at Helmstadt; his opinions on this subject appear in *De ludo litterario
recte aperiendo liber* (Rostock, 1597); for pertinent quotations from this work
see Reber, pp. 284 and 287.

33. John Caecilius Frey (*ca*. 1580–1631), born near Heidelberg; royal
physician and professor at Paris. The reference here is to his *Via Iani
Caecilii Frey ad divas scientias artesque, linguarum notitiam, etc*. For extensive
quotations from this work see Reber, p. 286.

34. Montaigne's father employed a German tutor who spoke Latin but
no French, with the result that young Michel learned Latin without the aid
of rules or textbooks and at the age of six could speak better Latin than
French. Cf. *Essais*, I, xxv.

only a few students could attend these institutions.[35] Ratke, whose program resembles that of Caselius, urges that a Latin author intelligible to youngsters—Terence, for example—be placed into the hands of pupils as soon as possible, so that by reading and rereading they may somehow begin to understand the language. He provides for no preliminary instruction in grammar but recommends that on the third reading a study should be made of the types of declensions and conjugations found in the text; thereafter phraseology and rules of syntax should be explained. The teacher should do almost all the work; the pupils should be enjoined to preserve Pythagorean silence. Ratke's method has found many supporters but also many opponents, notably Marius de Strachindis, who has shown that Ratke's method is basically wrong and only adds to the difficulties of the problem.[36]

Another approach is through the study of selected quotations. By providing fifteen sentences for memorizing each day, Vogelius attempts to introduce the beginner to the whole Latin vocabulary within one year; unfortunately, the quotations in his *Ephemerides*, chosen from sacred and profane writers, contain obsolete expressions and are not graded according to difficulty.[37] A better collection is that of Seidelius, whose *Portula* contains apt quotations carefully chosen from the best writers of Latin; this work, being systematically arranged in decades and centuries, is both pleasant and easy to use.[38]

35. Throughout his life Comenius devised many plans of education, but whatever his theory, his aim was always to educate the general public, not merely the chosen few.

36. For Ratke (Ratichius) see the *Analytical Didactic*, Axiom XXXIII, nn. 6 and 7 below, pp. 107–8.

37. Ezekiel Vogel of Holberg (*ca*. 1580–1643), director of the Gymnasium at Göttingen, published his *Ephemerides linguae Latinae* in 1620.

38. The *Portula Latinae* appeared in 1638 and by 1662 had gone through six editions; its author was Kaspar Seidel of Neudorf (*ca*. 1600–1660).

The present author must not fail to pay his respects to the Irish *Ianua linguarum;* he also wishes to show precisely in what way his own first *Ianua* of 1631 is related to the Irish *Ianua*. The latter work, first published by the Irish Jesuits in Spain,[39] consisted of twelve hundred sentences which would acquaint the student with a basic vocabulary in both Spanish and Latin because, except for such common words as *am, and, in,* each word appeared only once. In 1615 appeared a London edition of this work in a Latin-Spanish-English version and in 1617 another London edition in which French was added by Isaac Habrecht, who also produced the six-language Strassburg edition of 1624, in which he included German and Italian.[40] It is through this last version that the present author became acquainted with the work in 1628. Other noteworthy editions of the Irish *Ianua* are those of Scioppius, who published a Latin-Italian version of the text under the title *Mercurius bilinguis* (Milan, 1627) and a Latin-German-Greek-Hebrew version under the title *Mercurius quadrilinguis* (Basel, 1636).[41]

39. In 1611 at the Anglo-Irish college of Salamanca; the authors were William and John Bathe (Bateus) and Stephen White (P. Stephanus Hibernus).

40. Isaac Habrecht (*ca.* 1580–1633) was a physician and mathematician of Strassburg; he had become acquainted with the *Ianua* while on a visit to London.

41. Kaspar Schoppe (Scioppius) (1576–1649), German classical scholar; after conversion to Catholicism in 1598, he received the titles of *comes Palatinus* and count of Clara Valle; distinguished for his wide reading and remarkable memory; learned editor of Latin authors and witty writer of polemics against Scaliger, James I of England, and the Jesuits; author of many works on language, among them *Grammatica philosophica* (Milan, 1628) and *Auctarium ad Grammaticam philosophicam eiusque rudimenta* (Milan, 1629). From Scioppius we learn the names of the authors of the Irish *Ianua* (cf. chap. xxvii of *Methodus*, below), and it is to him that the Irish monk Stephen, when on the point of death in Madrid in 1614, intrusted this new method of teaching languages. In the Preface to his *De veteris ac novae grammaticae Latinae origine, dignitate et usu* Scioppius relates how as a boy of eight, without the aid of grammar but merely by listening and

Before 1628, when he became acquainted with the Irish *Ianua*, the present author had independently reached the conclusion, through his study of didactic principles, that words can best be taught in conjunction with things. He had also conceived a plan of giving simple instruction in Latin by means of a book which would present an orderly survey of all things and their properties. The book would endeavor to represent each thing and each attribute by the appropriate word; thus it would serve as a description of the totality of things and would reduce the whole fabric of language to one unbroken context. When he revealed this plan to his friends, the author was told that there already existed such a work with the title *Ianua linguarum*. At this news he leaped for joy, but, on examining the Irish *Ianua*, he discovered that it was not what he had hoped for.[42] He therefore decided to continue with his own project, and in 1631 he completed and published his work in Leszno under the title *Ianua linguarum reserata* ("The Gate of Languages Opened").[43] The book won a reception that was favorable beyond expectation; it has been translated into various European and even Asiatic languages and has been widely adopted in schools throughout Europe.[44]

But the author was not satisfied with the *Ianua*, for he soon came to realize that the work would be too difficult for

---

conversing, he acquired a mastery of Latin equal to that of his native German.

42. Because the book contained words too difficult for beginners and omitted many common words; each word appeared only once and therefore illustrated only one meaning; this meaning was not always the primary one; many of the sentences were awkward and meaningless.

43. This is the Latin version of the original Czech *Ianua*, which was also published in Leszno, but not until 1633.

44. For a survey of the complicated bibliographical history of this work see Appendix II. Keatinge (II, 310) notes that the *Ianua* was "published in Greek and Latin at Oxford as late as 1800; and in Latin, German, and Czech at Prague in 1874."

beginners; therefore, in the next year (1632) he prepared the
Vestibulum as an introduction to the *Ianua*. Later he
conceived the plan of arranging the whole study of languages into four convenient grades: the stammering, the
speaking, the fluent, and the eloquent. The existing *Vestibulum* and *Ianua* would serve as texts for the first two grades,
while a *Palatium* and a *Thesaurus* would supply material for
study in the last two grades.[45] The whole project, outlined in
the *Didactic Dissertation*,[46] met with the approval of many
learned men but was not brought to completion because "no
one moved a hand" to aid the author, and he himself was
occupied with other matters.

Meanwhile in 1634 Andrea Corvinus, professor of rhetoric
at Leipzig, announced his universal method for teaching
languages.[47] His plan was based on a universal grammar or
metaphysics of languages; after a general study of linguistic
structure one would proceed to the peculiarities of individual
languages, armed with an accurate and elaborate lexicon in
which primary words would be given first and then their
derivatives and compounds. Following a general survey of
words and the things for which they stand, one could read
literature intelligently and profitably.[48] A purely lexical

45. Elsewhere in the works of Comenius the *Palatium* is known as the
Atrium, and the *Thesaurus* as the *Palatium*. See Appendix II.

46. *De sermonis Latini studio, per vestibulum, ianuam, palatium, et thesauros
Latinitatis, quadripartito gradu plene absolvendo, didactica dissertatio* (Leszno,
1637). This work informs us that David Vechner, who in 1636 composed
Proplasma templi Latinitatis as a supplement to the fifth chapter of the
Ianua, was urged to continue his work but to rename it *Palatium*. Comenius
also requested Johannes Rave, professor of logic and director of schools in
Brandenburg, to compose a *Thesaurus;* neither task was accomplished.

47. In a letter to John M. Dilherr, professor of rhetoric at Jena and one
of the foremost Lutheran theologians and preachers of the day.—Reber,
p. 293.

48. At this point is quoted a passage from Corvinus which lists some of
the most important lexicons of the seventeenth century, e.g., the *Syllabus*

approach to the study of language is that of Engelbrecht, who published his *Compendisissima linguae Latinae methodus* in 1641. The first part of this work is a vernacular-Latin dictionary consisting of 3,661 Latin roots, while the second part lists derivatives and compounds arranged into twenty-two classes according to meaning.[49] It is difficult to see just how this work could be used to give instruction in a language.

The author has recently come upon *Consultationes de scholarum et studiorum ratione*, which Scioppius published in Padua in 1636. This work denounces the current method of teaching Latin, especially as practiced in Jesuit schools; it finds this method obscure, involved, and harmful to the study of the world of reality. Scioppius had tried to remedy these faults by devising a shorter and more pleasant way of acquiring a knowledge of Latin grammar through the study of Latin authors and for that purpose had published his *Grammatica philosophica* in Milan in 1628. The *Consultationes* is at once an argument for his own new method and a condemnation of traditional practices. These, with their burdensome and misleading instruction, render the mind unfit for an intelligent study of arts and letters; they overload it with rules and exceptions instead of making it an instrument for productive and socially useful thinking. Alvarus,[50] for instance, encumbers his *Syntaxis* with five hundred rules and a host of exceptions. Scioppius reduces all syntax to fifteen rules, with no exceptions.

---

of George Pasor and the *Lexicon* of John Starck. To a modern reader this passage is interesting because among these famous dictionaries is listed a *Hellas* of an Anton Lobegoys; neither the author nor the work is known to modern scholarship.

49. Jacob Engelbrecht of Stralsund was also the author of *Donatus seu progymnasmata*.

50. Manuel Alvarez (Alvarus) (1526–82), of Portugal; rector of the university at Coimbra; Jesuit grammarian; author of *Compendium grammaticae*, to which Comenius refers here as the *Syntaxis*.

Many other great scholars have sought for a method that would simplify the teaching of languages. Andrew Wilck (1562–1629), rector at Gotha, published his *Didactic*[51] in 1602. Christopher Helwig (Helvicius) (1581–1617), of Sprendling, professor of oriental languages at Giessen, helped to popularize Ratke's method in the *Kurtzer Bericht von der Didactica* . . . *Ratichii* (1614) and proposed a comprehensive method of teaching languages in *Libri didactici grammaticae universalis Latinae, Graecae, Hebraicae, Chaldaicae* (Giessen, 1619). Stephen Ritter (*ca.* 1600–1650) published a *Didactic* in 1621, and in the same year in Hamburg appeared the *Didactic* of Elias Bodin (*ca.* 1600–1650).[52] In 1622 Andrew Cramer published his work,[53] and in 1625 Statius Buscher (d. 1641), rector of the Hannover schools, published his *Disquisitio de recta iuventutis scholasticae institutione ad veram humanitatem et pietatem christianam*. In 1627 (1640) in Bremen appeared the *Schola privata* of Jacob Wolfstirn (*ca.* 1600–1660); and in 1628 Gabriel Holstein (1582–1649), the renowned Swedish linguist and professor of Greek at Westernäs, published certain specimens of what he calls the "divine Glaumian method."[54]

51. No longer extant.

52. Bodin's work was entitled *Bericht von der natur- und vernunfftmessigen Didactica oder Lehrkunst nebenst hellen und sonnenklaren Beweiss, etc.*, with the motto "Omnia faciliora facit ratio, ordo, et modus." In 1627 Comenius found this work in the library of Zilvar of Silberstein in Vlčice. The event had a far-reaching influence on his literary activities; Bodin's work inspired Comenius to compose the Czech *Didaktika*, the predecessor of the *Didactica magna*. Reber (p. 297) notes that Bodin also composed an *Ars mnemonica per imagines*.

53. Reber surmises that this work is *Anleitung, wie die Jugend in Gottesfrucht, Künsten und Sprachen zu unterweisen*. Cramer (1582–1640) was a theologian and a director of schools in Magdeburg.

54. One of the most fantastic educational nostrums of the age was this "Glaumian method," so called because it originated with a Frankfurt lawyer, Philip Glaum (*ca.* 1600–1650), who attracted much attention with a book bearing the remarkable title *Disputatio Castellani de methodo docendi artem*

The author has listed the preceding works in order to show that some of the most distinguished philologians of our time have sought to bring order out of confusion and that this century gives promise of finding a way out of our perplexities. Thus the present work follows in illustrious footsteps when it seeks to discover more efficient methods for solving a problem that urgently demands a solution.

Chapter ix.—We can end the present confusion in the teaching of languages if we adopt a method which will meet all requirements and answer all objections. Such a method, if it is to be satisfactory in every respect, must harmonize and incorporate the best counsels of the writers discussed in chapter viii. It must also utilize the latest theories and practices, so that it will be truly a *Methodus novissima*. This "newest" method must be brief and simple, free from error, devoid of prolixity, clear and attractive to the intelligence, and so general in scope that it can be applied to the study of all languages, sciences, and arts. Above all, this method must teach youngsters to examine words and things at the same time; since the structure of language parallels the structure of things, an understanding of the relations of words will bring with it an understanding of the relations of things.

Such a method can be achieved only on the basis of a correct didactics, which breaks down the barriers between minds and enables us to communicate knowledge to others. The unshakable basis of didactics is nature, and by nature's side stands art as an auxiliary, to guide us by rule and precept in handling whatever we teach and whomever we teach. Therefore, a truly universal method must be an art founded

---

quamvis intra octiduum (Giessen, 1621; Frankfurt, 1662). With the aid of this method a person might require six months to master Latin or Hebrew but only one month to learn Swedish or Italian. Unfortunately, I have not been able to examine Glaum's work.

on nature itself; it must be determined by what nature requires and allows.[55] A method so founded can provide a uniform technique which can be put to practical use not only in schools but in all other human activities that involve teaching and learning.

Our purpose, then, is to construct a didactics not merely for languages but for all human knowledge and action. "Let the reader note that in the *Didactica magna*[56] we probed the secret of this [didactic] art syncritically (comparatively); here we will undertake an analytical definition of this art, its aims, means, and modes of operation, in order to reveal its laws in a scientific (i.e., philosophic) way."[57]

Chapter x.—[This, the longest and the most elaborate chapter of the *Methodus*, has often been published separately under the title *Didactica analytica* and is the subject of the present translation. It consists of 160 sections devoted to an analytical exposition of didactic theories and techniques; it sums up in 187 axioms the fundamental principles that govern effective teaching. Sections 1–38 (Axioms I–LIV) constitute a general didactics of central guiding principles. Sections 39–128[58] (Axioms LV–CLVIII) deal with special problems; that is, subjects to be taught (Secs. 39–109), persons to be instructed (Secs. 110–23), and ends to be attained (Secs. 124–28). Sections 128–60 (Axioms CLIX–CLXXXVII) discuss specific procedures for achieving instruction that is rapid (Secs. 132–39), agreeable (Secs.140–49), and thorough (Secs. 150–60). The New Method of

55. Cf. Bacon's *Novum organum*, Aphorisms I, 3, and 129: "Nature to be commanded must be obeyed."—Spedding's translation.

56. Mainly in chaps. xvi–xviii; but see also Appendix I to the present volume.

57. The quoted passage, which serves to introduce the *Analytical Didactic*, was added at the end of this chapter in the second (Amsterdam) edition of the *Methodus*.

58. Secs. 39–127 in the Leszno edition.

teaching languages, developed in subsequent parts of the book, is based upon the principles outlined in this chapter.]

Chapter xi.—Our New Method, which is derived from the principles enunciated in chapter x and is elaborated in the remaining chapters of this work, has the virtue of being brief, simple, thorough, and correct. Its ultimate aim is to equip a student with a thorough knowledge of a language and a ready command of pure idiom, so that he will be able to speak and write fluently and correctly, even without the aid of grammars or dictionaries. This does not mean that he should learn every word in the language, for even Cicero did not know Latin in its entirety. Although the specialized vocabularies of various trades and professions have no place in our scheme, we must be ready to admit new words if they represent new things. Our main objective is to master the basic vocabulary, the general structure, and the useful idioms of a language.

Here, as in all other teaching, we must adapt our teaching to the native abilities and the maturity of our students; and we must proceed gradually and naturally, moving step by step from the simple to the complex. Therefore, our study should be divided into stages, and these should be taken up in the following order: (1) the fundamentals of the language; (2) the structure of the language; and (3) the power and the beauty of the language. A student must first build a solid foundation by acquiring a knowledge of root words and regular inflections. When he has learned these fundamentals of normal usage, he can proceed to the next step, that of combining words into properly constructed sentences. Only after he has mastered these first two steps can he attempt the use of special expressions and stylistic graces. If we proceed in this way, our method can become truly universal, that is, applicable to all languages.

Chapter xii.—The indicated goals can be achieved if both

teachers and pupils are provided with certain special instruments for the study of language: (1) texts dealing with
things; (2) lexicons interpreting the texts correctly; and
(3) grammars explaining the relations of words. Texts
supply examples, lexicons indicate usage, and grammars
supply precepts. The art of the New Method consists in a
skilful use of these instruments in combination. The supporting pillars of a language are good authors who deal with
good things in an orderly manner and thus provide us with a
systematic knowledge of life. In order to understand these
authors, we need brief and trustworthy lexicons, without
which the best authors remain foreigners speaking a foreign
tongue; and, in order to gain thorough understanding of any
language, we need grammars. But grammars are only
guides, and lexicons are merely aids to comprehension and
memory; they are not the masters of language but its servants.

Although complete mastery of a language comes only
from a study of the best authors—and for Latin the classic
authors are our only source of knowledge—the New Method
does not begin with a study of the classics. The secret of this
method lies in a gradual approach to the study of literature
by way of preparatory textbooks, carefully devised to open
up a short, dependable, and pleasant way to the reading of
standard authors. These artificially constructed textbooks,
built on uniform principles, will be graded according to the
level of the student's comprehension. They will contain
excerpts from the classics, a lexicon, and a grammar, all
suitable to the age, abilities, and understanding of the
student. Thus the student will have in front of him a text
which names things and explains them, on his left hand a
lexicon, and on his right hand a grammar. The lexicon will
serve as a bridge between meaning and mind; the grammar
will clarify the conventionally systematized relations of

words. Through these means we can erect an artificial ladder in which the sidepieces are things and words joined by the rungs of meaning.[59]

These preparatory textbooks will be the *Vestibulum*, the *Ianua*, and the *Atrium*, which constitute the way (*VIA*) to an intelligent study of language and literature. Each work will deal with the same matters but on successively more difficult levels. The *Vestibulum* will contain simple words, simple constructions, and regular inflections; its purpose is to lay a complete foundation for the study of language (1) by revealing to the beginner the most important objects in their natural order; (2) by acquainting him with the root words of a language; and (3) by teaching him regular declensions and conjugations. The *Ianua* will include a larger number of objects and will present the whole body and structure of the language, exclusive of figurative speech; its purpose is (1) to disclose more fully the connections of things in a natural order; (2) to unfold the main content or kernel of the language by fixing the root meanings of each word; and (3) to show the natural classes of Latin words, their forms and uses, as well as providing illustrative examples. The *Atrium* will introduce word formation (derivation and composition), periphrasis, and elegancies of style; its purpose is (1) to display things in borrowed robes, that is, to show how figurative and allegorical language is capable of renaming things and thus presenting them under varied aspects; (2) to give a systematic account of these verbal changes; and (3) to supply guiding precepts for the embellishment of the language and thereby reveal the very secret or inner spirit of the language. In short, the *Vestibulum* will disclose the skeleton of the language, the *Ianua* its body, and the *Atrium* its living colors. The method of the *Vestibu-*

59. A foretaste of the imagery if not the terminology of modern semantics.

lum will be analytic, that of the *Ianua* synthetic, and that of the *Atrium* syncritic.

Each of these three textbooks will be provided with its appropriate lexicon and grammar. These works will be written in a brief, simple, accurate style; whenever possible, they will make use of illustrations, since things themselves or pictures of things are far more instructive than the most accurate descriptions.[60] The composition of each work will follow the same plan: first the text, then the lexicon, and finally the grammar. In order to avoid duplication, the limits of each textbook will be strictly defined, so that one grade does not overlap into the next. By providing for such uniform and systematic progression, we avoid desultory and confused teaching which bewilders the student and places upon him a needless burden. Each book will also provide something especially attractive to the mind: for example, pictures in the text, parallels with the mother-tongue in the lexicon, and examples drawn from both languages to illustrate every rule in the grammar. Thus we can make the similarities and dissimilarities between languages immediately clear. A Latin-vernacular and a vernacular-Latin lexicon will be supplied for each of the three grades— vestibular, ianual, and atrial.[61]

Chapter xiii.—Instruments of instruction are useless unless one knows how to use them; hence the need of method and of enthusiastic teachers who know how to teach. Therefore, since the textbooks designed for the New Method are merely a specific and concrete application of the general principles developed in chapter x, those who use these text-

60. Direct evidence that the notion of using illustrations to enliven and clarify a text had been germinating in the author's mind long before the publication of the *Orbis pictus* (Nuremberg, 1658). Such illustrations had been suggested in 1617 by Eilhard Lubin; cf. chap. viii above.

61. See Appendix II for earlier plan of the *Ianua*, *Vestibulum*, and *Atrium*.

books must guide themselves by the rules set forth in that chapter. [Here follows a set of "practical" instructions on how to use the new textbooks; although most of these exhortations and caveats sound trite to modern ears, in the seventeenth century they had the ring of novelty.] Before textbooks are placed into the hands of pupils, all typographical errors should be corrected; teacher and pupils should have before them the same exemplars, which agree in every detail; instruction should be systematic and should progress by natural stages; pupils should understand a text before memorizing it, so that studies will strengthen the memory, not overburden and enfeeble it; since a pupil's attention and eagerness for learning are heightened by his participation in the activities of his fellows, pupils should not remain passive recipients of information but, by means of recitations and discussions, should take an active part in all instruction.

Chapter xiv.—Directions for the use of the text, lexicon, and grammar of the *Vestibulum linguarum novissimum* ("Newest Forecourt of Languages").[62] This new *Vestibulum*, composed according to the principles of the New Method, differs radically from the *Vestibulum* of 1633. The original work was made up of simple words arranged in short sentences which described the properties and activities of things under the daily observation of the young pupil. The new *Vestibulum*, in keeping with the axioms of chapter x, particularly Axiom CLIV, is designed to serve as an ample foundation for the whole structure of language-teaching. The text of this work will therefore contain all the root words of Latin, except for obscene terms, and will thus provide an introduction to the language as a whole.[63] It will

62. This work is printed in the *ODO*, II, 293, under the title *Vestibulum Latinae linguae, rerum et linguae cardines exhibens*.

63. The original *Vestibulum* contains 1,000 words in 427 sentences; the new *Vestibulum* contains 5,000 words. The *Vestibuli linguarum auctarium*

not arrange these words in sentences but will group them according to the logic of grammar and of reality, so that the study of language will go hand in hand with the study of things.[64] The text will begin with substantives grouped according to the most general concepts (e.g., "all—something—nothing"); then will follow the names of natural objects, artificial objects (products of arts and handicrafts), moral concepts, and spiritual concepts. After this will come words which describe actions and modes of action (verbs and the whole gamut of adverbial expressions). The lexicon will give an alphabetical list of all these words together with their translations into the vernacular; although it will consist chiefly of the root words of the language, it must inevitably include some derivatives and compounds. This lexicon will indicate the inflection of each word by supplying the genitive for declension and the infinitive, perfect, and future for conjugation. A reverse lexicon, from vernacular to Latin, should be constructed by the pupils themselves as their acquaintance with words increases. The grammar will not burden the novice's mind with definitions but will introduce him directly to regular declensions and conjugations. It will not deal with anomalous forms; nor will it attempt to expound the rules of accent for a language like Latin, which, unlike Greek and Bohemian, lacks diacritical marks. At the end of the grammar fifteen general rules will cover the subject of syntax. The work will close with a set of directions for the proper use of the *Vestibulum*.

Chapter xv.—Directions for the use of the text, lexicon, and grammar of the *Ianua linguarum novissima* ("Newest

---

of 1657, intended as a supplement to the new *Vestibulum*, composes these 5,000 words into 700 short sentences.

64. A clear example of the increased rigorism in the author's thinking; encyclopedic principles dominate these new textbooks. Even here, in the most elementary of these works, Comenius strives to inculcate a "logical" and pansophic view of the world.

Gate of Language").[65] The author is now ready to fulfil his promise of constructing a gate firmly set on the pillars of things, easily swung open on the hinges of a lexicon, and readily opened with the key of grammar. This new *Ianua*, because of its fuller and more accurate text, will differ markedly from the author's original *Ianua*, which represented and analyzed the world of things inadequately because it was composed on the principle that no word should be repeated.[66] By abandoning that false restriction ("superstition"), the new *Ianua* will be able to extend its scope. It will give the beginner an encyclopedic view of the arts and an epitome of the sciences; at the same time it will analyze subjects with greater precision than was possible in the original work. In further contrast to the earlier work, which was written with the Bohemian language in view, the new text will be composed in such a way that it can be adapted to any vernacular.[67] But the new *Ianua*, even though it adds sections on jurisprudence and theology,[68] cannot achieve the goal set up in chapter v above; it fails to supply a complete nomenclature of things (1) because the imperfect sci-

65. In *ODO*, II, 299, the title of this work is given as *Latinae linguae Ianua reserata, rerum et linguae structuram exhibens ordine nativo*.

66. As early as 1637, in Sec. 122 of the *Dissertatio didactica*, Comenius expressed his dissatisfaction with the original *Ianua* and promised a revised edition. In the Preface to the *Auctarium* (1657) he repudiated the original edition, together with all the imitations it had spawned, and expressed the wish to be judged by the second edition, which is substantially a new book. But it is the earlier version that made Comenius famous and continued to be the source of seventeenth- and eighteenth-century reprints and adaptations of the *Ianua*.

67. Although the earlier *Ianua* appeared in print for the first time as the Latin *Ianua linguarum* (Leszno, 1631), it had been originally composed in the Czech language.

68. At this point, in touching upon the major religious divisions of the world, Comenius declares that an Arabic version of the *Ianua* had pleased the Mohammedans and that the work had also been translated into Turkish, Persian, and Mongolian. For further details see chap. xxvii below.

ence of our day fails to provide a full analysis of the world; (2) because the extant body of Latin does not furnish a vocabulary sufficient to express existing knowledge; and (3) because, even if such an exhaustive vocabulary existed in Latin, it could not be rendered into any vernacular language.

Although the new work will retain the original plan of one thousand sentences arranged in hundreds, the text will be fuller, its exposition more lucid, and its subdivisions more logical and more natural. It will maintain parallelism between things and words and will illustrate all grammatical constructions, every variety of phrase, and every kind of sentence structure. Thus, except for rhetorical figures, it will serve as a compact grammar and a concrete illustration of all etymological, syntactical, prosodic, and orthographic rules.

The lexicon is specifically designed as a glossary for the *Ianua*, not as a general dictionary. Since our objective is not facile instruction in what things are but an education based on the scrutiny of why things are what they are, the lexicon is not intended for ready reference but for etymological study.[69] Therefore, it will group words according to their roots, relate each word to its paronyms, and distinguish it from its homonyms. This lexicon will also provide an analytic, synthetic, and syncritic approach to the study of words by presenting its materials in three columns: (1) Latin words listed according to roots; (2) their counterparts in the vernacular; and (3) sentences in which Latin words are used in combination with their paronyms. Pupils can exercise their skill and ingenuity by devising their own vernacular-Latin glossary for the *Ianua*.

The grammar should win general commendation because

69. Unfortunately, Comenius' whole etymological system is wrong because he derives Latin from Greek and Greek from Hebrew.

it will be eminently simple yet complete enough to reveal the whole structure of the language. It will merely amplify and illustrate the general outlines of the vestibular grammar and will stress only essentials, but it will be sufficiently full to enable anyone to read, speak, and write the language. In order to avoid the inaccuracies and obscure subtleties of many earlier grammatical works, it will proceed according to philosophical principles. Its rules will derive from logic, even as the rules of logic derive from things themselves; for the basis of speech is thought, and the basis of thought is the thing itself.[70] In keeping with Axiom XLI of chapter x, this grammar will be arranged in three columns: (1) examples; (2) precepts; and (3) references to illustrative passages in the text of the *Ianua*. Only one example will illustrate each rule; the pupil can exercise his diligence by searching out further examples in the text. The author hopes that this textbook will be a source of pleasure and a gateway to loftier intellectual undertakings.

Chapter xvi.—Sketch of the *Atrium linguarum novissimum* ("Newest Entrance Hall of Languages").[71] The *Atrium* will deal with such rhetorical variations as figurative speech and

70. In all his theorizing about grammar Comenius is dominated by this analogist view of language. Reber notes (pp. 417–18) that in this chapter Comenius' observations on grammar are largely influenced by the writings of Vossius, particularly *De vocum analogia et anomalia* and *Aristarchus sive de arte grammatica*.

71. This work was not completed until the Sáros Pátak period (1650–54). Pars. 22 and 24 in chap. xxii of the *Didactica magna* (written 1633–38) give a brief sketch of such a work under the title *Palatium* ("Palace of Latin Authors"), and Secs. 68–91 of the *Dissertatio didactica* (1637) outline its general scheme. In the *Methodus* Comenius changed the title *Palatium* to *Atrium* but evidently did not compose more than a sketch of the work; hence the merely general discussion of its contents in the present chapter. The Atrium was finally published in 1652 under the title *Eruditionis scholasticae pars tertia: Atrium rerum et linguarum ornamenta exhibens*. It was reprinted in the *ODO*, Part III, in 1657; another reprint, authorized by Comenius in 1655, was published in 1659 by Endter in Nuremberg.

skilful paraphrase. This treatise may seem of doubtful value, since language poses enough difficulties without the aid of such purely ornamental complications. Words have become so blurred in meaning that they no longer correspond to things, with the result that this Babylonian confusion of language forms a barrier between our intelligence and the world of reality. Hence the justness of the demand that, instead of cultivating verbal ornament and elaborate diction, we should strive to reduce language to utter simplicity and literalness.[72] But, despite frequent misuse, rhetorical ornament has its proper uses. The human mind consists not only of an intellect that is to be instructed but also of a will that is susceptible to the charms of rhetoric. Man desires not only truth but also beauty; therefore, it is important to make truth attractive. Furthermore, when a thing is not intelligible in itself, it must be illustrated by means of another; hence the need of figurative speech. Finally, wisdom has always made use of symbolic utterance; from the earliest antiquity men have sought to comprehend the universe by translating it into symbols, that is, by comparing the unknown to the known. Hence the wealth of images in the ancient writers. Since our aim is to enable the student to read and readily comprehend these classics, the inclusion of the *Atrium* in the *Methodus* is clearly justified.

Like the *Ianua*, the *Atrium* will consist of a text, a grammar, and a lexicon; that is, in accordance with Axiom XL in chapter x, it will organize the teaching of rhetorical devices into examples, precepts, and exercises. The subjects and the arrangement of those subjects in the atrial text will be the same as in the ianual text, but the treatment will be fuller and the expression more elaborate, since rhetorical adornment will be freely introduced. Literal and direct phrasing

72. Comenius himself was an ardent seeker for a clear and logical means of universal communication.

will give place to the oblique language of rhetorical discourse in order to heighten the attractiveness, pleasure, and usefulness of instruction. The text will give copious illustrations of tropes and figures, idiomatic Latin expressions, conventional phrases, and proverbial sayings; it will also provide examples of the two great styles of Latin prose, the Asiatic and the laconic.[73]

The atrial grammar will supplement the ianual grammar, especially in the treatment of such constructions as make for elegance and subtlety of expression; it will also teach the student how to analyze the devices of Latin rhetoric and how to appropriate them for his own use.

The atrial lexicon will be a vernacular-Latin and a Latin-vernacular index to phrases and proverbial expressions. By adding a Latin-Latin lexicon in which simple expressions appear side by side with their elegant variants, the author hopes to instruct the student in the art of paraphrasing bald statements and thus teach him how to cultivate various literary styles.[74]

Chapter xvii.—The New Method applied to the reading of Latin authors.[75] The *Vestibulum, Ianua,* and *Atrium* teach a student to understand, write, and speak Latin, but they are merely skeletal works, artificial short cuts. He who would

73. I.e., the Ciceronian and the Senecan or Lipsian.

74. The atrial lexicon was not printed until 1657, by John Jansson in Amsterdam, when Comenius was residing in that city; it was not included in the *ODO* of 1657, which was published by Christopher Cunrad and Gabriel Roy.

75. We have no work of Comenius which embodies the suggestions given in the present chapter. This last grade in the study of language is discussed under the title *Thesaurus Latinitatis* ("Treasury of Latin") in Secs. 92–121 of the *Dissertatio didactica* of 1637, where Comenius recommends the study of all subjects and all varieties of discourse as they are treated by ancient and modern writers in physics, geography, ethics, medicine, politics, theology, history, oratory, and poetry. Sections 23 and 24 of chap. xxii in the *Didactica magna* also give a brief outline of this *Thesaurus*. See Appendix II.

know Latin as a real and living language must read Latin authors, for they are the only true source of Latin. Real learning and eloquence cannot be acquired except through the reading and rereading of Latin historians, orators, poets, philosophers, theologians, and writers on medicine and jurisprudence. These give the student a broad and thorough acquaintance with the rich contents and the varied styles of a great literature, but, above all, they teach him wisdom. No one author can suffice, for not even Cicero has written on all subjects or exhausted the riches of his language. But it does not follow that we must read all authors; careful selection is always necessary. Nor should we read most authors merely for their style. As Erasmus wisely suggests, it is advisable not to linger over books for the sake of scrutinizing their diction, but, once the language has been mastered, to undertake the reading of authors who deal with "realities." Or, as Vossius puts it, in the tree of learning we should seek the fruit of things, not the foliage of words.[76]

To acquire an adequate nomenclature of things, we should read Pliny for arts and sciences, Vitruvius for architecture, Vegetius and Caesar for military affairs, Celsus for medicine, and Varro and Columella for husbandry.[77] If we wish to acquire a command of conversational phrases and everyday expressions, Plautus and Terence will serve best. Letter-writers and historians will furnish patterns of the lower and the middle style; poets and orators will teach us sublimity. Cicero is the best model for the ornate style, as Seneca is for

76. For Erasmus the author refers us to *De ratione studii* and for Vossius to *De vitiis sermonis glossematis*, Book ii, chap. 27.

77. Pliny the Elder, *Historia naturalis* (37 books); Marcus Vitruvius Pollio, *De architectura libri x;* Vegetius Renatus, *Epitome institutionum rei militariae libri v;* Aurelius Cornelius Celsus, *De medicina* (8 books); Marcus Terentius Varro, *De re rustica libri iii;* Lucius Iunius Moderatus Columella, *De re rustica libri xii.* Compare Milton's list in *Of Education* (1644) and the much more comprehensive program in Vives, *De disciplinis* (1531), Book iv.

the laconic. In choosing examples of poetic style, we need not seek beyond Virgil for the heroic, Ovid for the elegiac, and Horace for the lyric.

In keeping with the general plan of the New Method, these texts will be read with the aid of a specially designed lexicon and a grammar that will provide extensive opportunity for individual practice.

The lexicon will be an encyclopedic dictionary (*repertorium catholicum*) containing (1) words not found in the *Ianua* or *Atrium*; (2) historical, geographical, scientific, religious, mythological, and literary terms and allusions; and (3) abbreviations. This mercury will facilitate the reading of the texts by giving an immediate explanation of every reference and allusion.[78] Excellent dictionaries of such general scope have been prepared by the brothers Stephanus,[79] and there are also special dictionaries for philosophy, medicine, law, and theology. But none of these works serves the purpose of our method. We require a lexicon which contains all extant words, even those found only in rare books, whether ancient or modern.[80] This lexicon will omit all words previously listed in the *Ianua* and the *Atrium*, for otherwise it would be needlessly ponderous. It will be carefully arranged so as to facilitate ready reference.

The New Method will furnish precepts on how a student can make practical use of his reading.[81] These rules will teach

78. *Mercurius* is a common seventeenth-century name for an encyclopedic dictionary.

79. The reference is to the famous *Thesaurus linguae Latinae* of Robert Étienne (1503–59) and to the *Dictionarium historico-geographicum-poeticum* of Charles Étienne (1504–64).

80. Comenius observes that the Englishman Rider (Bishop John Rider [1562–1632]) had attempted such a dictionary and that this work, if properly supplemented, would be the most comprehensive dictionary in existence. According to Reber (p. 426), Comenius had become acquainted with Rider's *Dictionarium Anglo-Latinum* during the visit to England in 1641–42.

81. This compendium of rules was intended to correspond to the grammars of the vestibular, ianual, and atrial grades.

him how to discover and how to imitate the hidden art used in the composition of epistles, histories, orations, and poems. Since imitation without analysis produces only blind copying, the New Method will provide guidance for individual practice in analyzing a writer's work, making excerpts from it, and imitating it intelligently.

To understand a work properly, we must first determine the author's purpose and then carefully examine his methods of selecting and arranging materials for that purpose. It is also instructive to transfer to a commonplace book any passages rich in matter or skilful in phrasing or in reasoning, for no man can become learned or eloquent without such aids to memory. But the most important aid in the development of a good style is continued and painstaking imitation of a good writer. The question of whether we should use authors as models or whether we should imitate only nature has exercised many great minds. As Stewichius has shown, this problem bred learned disputes between Angelus Politianus and Paulus Cortesius, Erasmus and Stephanus Doletus and J. C. Scaliger, Franciscus Picus Mirandulanus and Petrus Bembus.[82] The New Method resolves this controversy.

82. From among the numerous writings of these authors, Reber (p. 428) cites the works pertinent to this dispute; the present note makes use of Reber's citations. Stewichius Godescalcus of Holland (*ca.* 1520–90), professor at Point à Mousson in Lorraine, author of *De particulis linguae Latinae*, wrote commentaries on Vegetius, Frontinus, Apuleius, and Arnobius. Angelo Poliziano (Politianus) (1454–94), Italian humanist, poet, protégé of Lorenzo de' Medici, teacher of Greek in Florence, author of *Miscellanea* (critical essays), translated into Latin the *Iliad* (Books 2–5), Herodian, Epictetus' *Encheiridion*, and Plato's *Charmides*. Paulus Cortesius (1465–1510) of Dalmatia, bishop of Urbino, author of an exposition of Peter Lombard's *Sentences*, esteemed for the excellence of his Latin style. Desiderius Erasmus of Rotterdam (1467–1536), polyhistor and philologian, author of *Dialogus de recta Latini Graecique sermonis pronuntiatione*, *De ratione studii ac legendi interpretandique autores*, *Tractatus de pueris instituendis*, *Epistolae ad Longolium*, and *Ciceronianus sive de optimo dicendi genere*. Étienne Dolet (Stephanus Doletus) of Orléans (1509–46), painter and philologist, author of *Commentarii de lingua Latina libri ii*, *Formulae locutionum Latinarum illustriorum*,

According to Axioms XLI and CXXXIV in chapter x, one cannot learn except from an exemplar; but one need not be perpetually bound to exemplars. After a student has firmly established habits of good workmanship, he can work independently (Axiom CL). In other words, the imitation of models is a necessary step to independent composition.

The method of imitation is threefold. First comes reciprocal metaphrase, whereby we translate from Latin into the vernacular and after a few days recast our translation into Latin so as to see how close we can come to the original and how well we have mastered the author's phraseology. Another method is to translate Latin into Latin by rearranging, abridging, or amplifying a text and then to turn the new version back into the original form. Finally, there is imitation proper, a mode of composition in which we treat a subject drawn from our own experience but develop it in the manner of the author whom we are striving to emulate. Through diligent practice in this kind of judicious imitation we readily gain an intimate acquaintance with the classics and acquire purity of taste. We must, however, cultivate only one author at a time in order to avoid confusion of styles. Furthermore, we should practice daily so as to assure steady progress, and we should always proceed from the less difficult to the more difficult, from short pieces to longer ones. But in this preoccupation with technique we must not

---

and *Dialogus de imitatione Ciceroniana pro Longolio contra Erasmum*, a work which involved him in a controversy with Scaliger; he was a leader of the early sixteenth-century intellectual Renaissance and was burned at the stake in Paris for atheism. J. C. Scaliger (1484–1558), the great Italian philologian, author of the *Poetics* and *Orationes duae pro Cicerone contra Ciceronianum Erasmi*. Francesco Pico della Mirandola (Mirandulanus) (1469–1533), nephew of the more famous Giovanni, philosopher and literary scholar, author of *De imitatione*, distinguished for his wide learning. Cardinal Bembo (Petrus Bembus) (1470–1547), born in Venice, polymath and patron of Greek scholars who had fled from Constantinople to Italy; among his many works the most pertinent here is *De imitatione sermonis Marci Tullii*.

become enamored of mere style. We must never forget that words without matter are empty and that the manner of Cicero or Seneca is less important than the substance. Our main concern should be not with words but with things.

Chapter xviii.—The special merits of the New Method.[83] Our method excels in three respects: (*a*) by maintaining complete parallelism between words and things, it gives practical instruction in language and at the same time cultivates the mind; (*b*) by avoiding all coercion, it encourages spontaneous endeavor; and (*c*) by providing agreeable individual practice, it banishes apathy and arouses enthusiasm for the work in hand. Finally, the New Method is distinguished by its universality; it can be adapted to all subjects, all minds, all nations; it can be used for rapid, agreeable, and thorough instruction not only in Latin but also in Greek, Hebrew, and Arabic, as well as in the arts and sciences. Specifically this universal method can be applied to nine distinct uses:

1. To make the use of Latin more widespread among all nations.
2. To make the study of Latin an introduction to a more efficient cultivation of the vernacular.
3. To promote polyglot knowledge.
4. To promote factual knowledge of every sort.
5. To bring about an easier, better, and truer understanding of holy scripture.
6. To instil prudence as a by-product of other mental activities.
7. To improve the organization of all schools.
8. To bring about a general improvement in the state of learning.
9. To aid the spread of culture among uncivilized nations and to bring about a measure of universal agreement on many points.[84]

83. In this chapter Comenius shows in detail how his method will more than satisfy the demands of the writers whose theories were discussed in chap. viii above.

84. Each of these nine points is developed in a separate chapter below; see chaps. xix–xxvii.

Chapter xix.—The problem of teaching Latin more expeditiously to all nations and of providing special means to that end. It is desirable, as chapter vi makes clear, that Latin should become the universal language of the world. The difficulty of teaching the language, especially under widely varying conditions, is largely removed by the New Method, which, because of its carefully graded textbooks, can be readily adapted to every kind of instruction. It can be used by the public schools for commoners, by the private schools for the aristocracy, as well as by self-taught men. Of course we could greatly facilitate the study of Latin by establishing colleges in which Latin would be used not only for academic exercises but also for the commonest tasks of everyday life. But under all conditions, in all countries, in school or out of school, the New Method can be put to effective use because the vestibular, ianual, and atrial textbooks can be adapted to the study of any language and any culture. Essentially the same texts, since these contain a full nomenclature of things, can be used anywhere; the lexicons and the grammars, however, will have to be somewhat modified to satisfy the particular needs of various languages.[85] But, if we are going to make Latin understood among all nations, we shall first have to adopt one standard pronunciation of the language. The present regional differences are so great that even learned men, if they come from different countries, cannot understand one another's spoken Latin.

Chapter xx.—Latin as a guide to the cultivation of the vernacular. The New Method can serve as a gateway to the study of the speech of any nation because the graded curriculum which it provides for the study of Latin can be

85. Comenius, like most of his European contemporaries, did not realize how radical are the structural differences between the language systems of the world.

adapted to instruction in any language. The author fully
realizes that it is no easy task to prepare vestibular, ianual,
and atrial textbooks for languages that stem from widely
differing cultures.[86] Deficiencies in vocabulary and idiom
make it difficult to establish parallels between languages;
the Brazilians, for instance, have no word for God, and the
Abyssinians call their emperor "precious John."[87] Even
Latin does not have a complete fund of words. But borrowings from foreign languages together with compounds, new
coinages, and new formations based on the native stock can
raise any language to the level of more cultivated tongues.[88]
Furthermore, each language has its own peculiar devices for
rendering clearly and expressively the parallel idioms of
other languages. It is important to cultivate and to explore
these resources of native speech because the mother-tongue
is a primary tool for acquiring knowledge and because the
study of the mother-tongue is a valuable aid to the study of
Latin, for a student can learn the mysteries of grammar
more easily in a language he knows than in a language of
which he is ignorant.[89]

Chapter xxi.—The New Method as an aid to polyglot learning. The mastery of several languages is a glorious but rare
achievement; even among the Romans, as Alsted relates,[90]

86. A large part of this chapter is devoted to an account of the peculiarities of Greek, Latin, German, Polish, Czech, Hebrew, and Hungarian.

87. *Prêto-Jan* (Prester John), which Comenius derives from *pretiosus Johannes;* he rejects the correct explanation (Old French *Prestre Jean,* from
Presbyter Johannes) as "contrary to reason and truth." This whole chapter
illustrates the seventeenth-century "rational" approach to linguistic study.

88. Comenius shared with the members of the Pléiade this Renaissance
desire to embellish ("illustrate") the vernacular.

89. Thus a chapter intended to show how Latin can be a gateway to the
study of the vernacular ends with a plea for the study of the vernacular as an
introduction to Latin.

90. John Henry Alsted (1588–1638), the learned teacher at Herborn who
first aroused Comenius' interest in pansophy and encyclopedic learning. In

Cato's knowledge of merely three languages was considered remarkable. To learn a new language is difficult (1) because language embraces the whole realm of knowledge; (2) because there is no essential connection between words and the things they represent; and (3) because there is no fixed correlation between languages unless they have a common origin. The New Method disposes of some of these obstacles by introducing a parallelism between words and things and also by providing a lexicon and a grammar which can be adapted to any language. Our method also reduces difficulties by calling for a systematically graduated course of study and by requiring that only one language be studied at a time. We cannot agree with the proposal of Erasmus that Latin and Greek be studied together;[91] nor do we approve polyglot editions of our own *Ianua* and *Vestibulum*, because a text in many languages merely confuses a student. Indeed, such lexicons as the *Calepinus* published in eleven languages serve more for show than for use.[92] Comparative lexicons and comparative grammars are of little value to the student, who usually has enough trouble mastering one language. Of course such works can be used to advantage by scholars

---

the *Scientiarum omnium encyclopaedia* (Herborn, 1629), Book xxiv, chap. iv, Alsted remarks that Ennius considered Cato's knowledge of Latin, Oscan, and Greek as something of a miracle (see Reber, pp. 453, 492). For Alsted's influence on Comenius and on the age in general see P. R. Cole, *A Neglected Educator: Johann Heinrich Alsted* (Sydney, Australia, 1910), and Max Lippert, *Johann Heinrich Alsteds pädagogisch-didaktische Reform-Bestrebung und ihr Einfluss auf J. A. Comenius* (Meissen, S.A., 1898).

91. At the beginning of the *De ratione studii*.

92. In the seventeenth century the term *calepinus* or *calepin* was a common name for a dictionary. Ambrosius Calepinus (Calepino) (1435–1511), Italian lexicographer and Augustinian monk, published his Latin-Italian *Lexicon Latinum* in 1502. This work was expanded into many polyglot versions and was re-edited as late as 1771 under the title *Totius latinitatis lexicon*, the posthumous work of Forcellini. Commenius' reference is to the eleven-language edition of 1590.

who wish to extend their research into the nature and the development of human speech. The volumes of Martinius, Hayne, and Gelenius attest how this synoptic approach to language can add to our knowledge of language and of things themselves.[93] Inquiries of such wide scope can be a source of delight and instruction because they enable us to contemplate and better understand the wonders of creation. But we must temper our enthusiasm for languages, because polyglot learning may only confuse or stupefy the mind. Let us not squander mental capacities on language but reserve them for the more useful study of things.

Chapter xxii.—The value of the New Method for the study of *realia.*[94] The study of language should not be an end in itself but should lead to the study of things, for wisdom consists in the knowledge of things, not words.

The New Method can be readily adapted to the study of all arts and sciences. Any course of study, whether in philosophy, medicine, jurisprudence, or theology, can be subdivided into the graduated steps which the method pro-

93. Matthias Martinius (1572–1630), rector of the Bremen Gymnasium; author of *Lexicon philologicum.* Thomas Hayne (1581–1645), London schoolmaster whom Comenius probably met in England; the reference here is to Hayne's *Linguarum cognatio seu de linguis in genere et de variarum linguarum cognatione dissertatio* (London, 1639). Sigismundus Gelenius (Zikmund Jelenský) (1477–1554), Czech humanist, born in Praha; learned Greek in Venice and Bologna; became director of the scholarly Froben press in Basel, where he annotated and edited Greek and Latin classics; his *Dictionarium quadrilingue* (Latin-German-Slavic-Greek), which Comenius terms *Lexicon symphonicum,* was published in 1537 and was particularly notable because it contained a Czech section (see Reber, p. 456).

94. This chapter clearly reveals the pansophic bias of the author's mind. While ostensibly preparing a set of textbooks for the study of language, Comenius is endeavoring to develop a system of tabulating all knowledge and for discovering the Baconian *filum labyrinthi* that would lead men out of dark confusion into the realm of light. His belief that chaos must yield to order predetermines his conceptions in linguistics, science, and religion; it also provides the basis for his unshakable faith in the validity of his irenic endeavors. See Appendix III.

vides. Once the objectives have been determined, the whole process of instruction can be strictly organized so that each operation will fall into place. Simple beginnings will lead to more and more complex matters, until the whole structure of the subject stands fully revealed. For each course of study we can devise a series of vestibular, ianual, and atrial texts in which the method of teaching by example, precept, and practice can be applied throughout. As in language so in the arts and sciences we can proceed from rudiments to more advanced studies and finally to complete mastery. Such a natural progression is possible even in religions instruction. Just as the study of Latin, according to our method, finally brings us to the reading of Latin authors, so the study of divine matters will lead us to the reading of divine authors, those amanuenses of the Holy Spirit, the prophets and the apostles. Although all our reading should always be thorough and never cursory, let us remember that, in reading the works of men, we must not surrender our minds to any man. Authors should be guides, not dictators; they ought to sharpen the mind, not enslave it.

Chapter xxiii.—The value of the New Method for an easier, truer, and better understanding of Divine Scripture. The word of God has been given to all but is not read or understood by all men. It is our pious intent that the New Method may be used to promote the knowledge of the sacred texts. In the first place, since the method can be extended to the study of all languages, it will enable students to penetrate to the very sources of Holy Writ by way of Hebrew, the language of the prophets, and by way of Greek, the language of the apostles. Second, our method of studying words as parallel to things is particularly well adapted to the study of Holy Writ, because the whole Bible is one extended parable which speaks of the abstruse and the invisible in words designating the obvious and the visible.

Finally, our program of graded textbooks can also be employed profitably in the study of the Bible. We can prepare a *Vestibulum* of short and simple excerpts from the Scriptures and then a *Ianua* consisting of all the essential biblical texts but omitting repetitions and genealogical, geographical, and historical digressions. We can do this without injury to the meaning of the Bible, as our Czech epitome bears witness.[95] The *Atrium* could take the form of an emblem book in which the text of the Bible would be adorned with ingenious illustrations.[96] These pictures would delight the faithful, and, by making the proverbial sayings of the Bible clear and vivid, they would also help to explain the meaning of many a difficult passage. But the best commentary on the Bible is the Bible itself. The New Method supplies the means for a brief, lucid, and solid exposition of the biblical text; it furnishes the apparatus for comparing parallel passages from the Bible, for interpreting them in the light of reason, and for demonstrating the truth of Holy Writ by showing how the words of God correspond to the things that we perceive with our senses.

95. The author refers to his Czech *Manuálník*, an abbreviated text of the Bible. This work had been completed by 1623 but was not published until 1658 in Amsterdam. Its Latin counterpart appeared in Nuremberg in 1658 under the title *Ianua sive introductorium in Biblia sacra*. Also in Nuremberg in 1658 appeared Comenius' *Novi Testamenti epitome, typorum diversitate res, verba, phrases, atque sententias exhibens*.

96. Such emblem books, containing symbolic illustrations interpreted by accompanying verses, had been extremely popular in Europe ever since the Italian jurist Andrea Alciati (1492–1550) had published his collection of illustrated moral Latin sayings in the *Emblematum libellus* (1522). This work was translated into French, Italian, and Spanish; it was also widely imitated: e.g., Gabriel Rollenhagen's *Nucleus emblematum selectissimorum* (1610–13), the Jesuit Herman Hugo's *Pia desideria* (Antwerp, 1624), and the *Typus mundi* (1627) published by the Jesuits of Antwerp. Edmund Spenser shows the influence of Alciati in the closing stanzas of the *Ruines of Time*, but the best-known examples of this genre in England are Francis Quarles's *Emblems* (1635) and George Wither's Collection of *Emblemes* (1634–35).

Chapter xxiv.—The value of the New Method for instilling prudence and correcting faulty behavior. With the ancients, we believe that virtue can be taught; hence our method provides guidance for wise and prudent conduct. Since our main objective is not to give training in particular skills but to cultivate the mind and to inculcate habits which will become second nature, we have based the New Method on principles that are universally valid and therefore can be readily translated into modes of intelligent behavior. Whoever consistently applies these principles in his studies forms the habit of always keeping the chief goal in view, of selecting means conducive to a desired end, of proceeding gradually and systematically, of avoiding desultory effort, of referring all theory to practice, of pursuing his task briskly and energetically, of rigorously following well-defined precepts, of submitting to mild and helpful discipline, of acknowledging error and correcting it immediately, of testing his knowledge in open discussion, of supplying deficiencies in his knowledge through frank inquiry, and of resolving his doubts by balancing reason against reason. A valuable aid to prudent conduct can be supplied by a commonplace book of appropriate maxims and observations drawn from one's reading and daily discourse.

Chapter xxv.—The value of the New Method for improving the organization of our schools. Wide public dissatisfaction with current educational systems has produced demands for general reform. That the New Method has something to offer in the way of bringing about desired reforms will be apparent to anyone who considers the proposals which we have made thus far.

The assumptions on which we base our method stem from our notion of what constitutes the best kind of school. A school is a workshop in which humanity is molded. Since the proper functions of humanity are reason (RATIO), speech

(ORATIO), and action (OPERATIO), it follows that the purpose
of a school is to cultivate these functions in man, that is, to
teach him how to know (*Sapere*), act (*Agere*), and speak
(*Loqui*); these are the activities which yield the divine salt
(SAL) of education. The word "school" (SCHOLA) is in itself
symbolic of the sixfold purpose of a school:[97]

1. *S*		1. *Sapienter*	wisely
2. *C*		2. *Cogitare,*	to think,
3. *H*		3. *Honeste*	honestly
	should teach		
4. *O*		4. *Operari,*	to work,
5. *L*		5. *Loqui*	to speak
6. *A*		6. *Argute*	sagaciously

Furthermore, the double meaning of the word *ludus* ("play"
and "school") is a reminder that play should form an
integral part of school activity.

The New Method furnishes the implements needed in this
workshop of culture and teaches their use through constant
practice. A school conducted on the principles of our method
combines instruction with play and allows for proper relaxa-
tion. It gives full scope to intellectual and physical activity;
encourages spontaneous effort as an exercise of human
liberty; demands social and co-operative endeavor; nour-
ishes honest rivalry; insists upon well-regulated competition
and fair play; requires constant practice with a minimum of
theory and abstract discussion; lays stress upon direct observation and upon learning through sense impressions; and
enjoins moderation in work and play while providing suffi-

97. Reber (p. 481) notes the use of a similar acrostic in John Henry
Alsted's *Encyclopaedia*, Book xxxi, chap. vii, "Mnemonica": "*S*apienter
*C*ogitandum, *H*oneste *O*perandum, *L*iberaliter *A*gendum." These word
games, to which the contemporaries of Comenius were much addicted, are
sometimes used only as mnemonic devices, but often accidental parallels,
fanciful resemblances, strained analogies, and fantastic "etymologies" mas-
querade as evidence and reasoning.

ciently varied occupations to prevent weariness and boredom. A school with such a well-regulated discipline relieves
the teacher of drudgery, rescues him from boredom, and
permits him to give his full attention to the intellectual and
moral welfare of his charges.

Chapter xxvi.—The value of the New Method for improving the present state of learning. The schools of today suffer
from a scarcity of learned men. Although we have succeeded
in multiplying the number of our schools, we have failed to
produce the learned and cultivated teachers needed to make
these schools a source of profit and delight. The printing
press has made books readily available and has thereby en-
couraged private reading. For this reason and also because
of the harsh and grinding discipline in our schools, enthusiasts for learning have taken refuge in solitary study.
Such self-education, when based on unselected and un-
systematic reading, leads to unbalanced, lopsided learning
and uncouth pedantry. It often produces erudition but
rarely culture, for many an erudite volume harbors a rude
spirit.

The New Method, since it avoids severe and oppressive
discipline and makes no exorbitant demands upon the
memory, will open up the treasuries in which learning is
held captive. Because of its insistence upon individual practice and independent observation of phenomena and also
because of its universal outlook, its thoroughness, its broad
scope, its reasonableness, and its moderation, our method
will counteract the verbalism, servile imitation, parrotry,
narrowness, superficiality, one-sidedness, harshness, quarrel-
someness, and moroseness of the present systems in which
crude and boorish teachers terrorize stupefied and stultified
pupils. Just as the art of printing has facilitated, standard-
ized, and improved the production of books, so the New
Method will disseminate learning, purify it, refine it, and

make it available to the less gifted as well as to the more richly endowed.

Chapter xxvii.—The value of the New Method for spreading culture among uncivilized nations and for bringing about a measure of universal concord. Human nature is the same everywhere but sometimes appears barbarous because some men have not had the opportunity to become civilized. Their minds, their language, and their manners are rude because they have been taught no better. Given the proper guidance, they will become reasonable and intelligent in thought, speech, and behavior. By simplifying the teaching of languages and thereby expediting communication, the New Method may prove to be a potent force in this civilizing process, because language, being a repository of the refinements, wisdom, and virtue of more cultivated peoples, is a medium through which a higher culture can be readily transmitted to less civilized nations.

The author has special reasons for believing that his reforms in the teaching of languages may lead to a better understanding among peoples of different cultures and faiths. In 1642 in Leyden he met Jacobus Golius, whose brother Peter had translated the *Ianua* into Arabic.[98] According to a letter which Jacobus had received from his brother in Aleppo, the Mohammedans had been so pleased with the Arabic version of the *Ianua* that they had commissioned a group of scholars to translate it into Turkish, Persian, and Mongolian.[99] This success in overcoming the barriers of language and in achieving harmony in elementary studies gives rise to the hope that we can achieve harmony

98. Jacob van Gool (Golius) (1596–1667), professor of oriental languages at Leyden and author of *Lexicon Arabico-Latinum*, had traveled in Asia Minor. Peter van Gool, a convert to Catholicism, became a Carmelite and spent many years in Lebanon and Syria; in his later years he became professor of oriental languages in Rome.

99. Cf. chap. xv above, n. 68.

in the weightier matter of bringing about a common understanding among nations. Disputes and dissensions are largely the result of verbal disagreements.[100] The New Method,
which relates the study of words to the study of things, reveals how direct observation of things dispels the quarrels
that thrive on verbalism. In other words, our method can
help Truth shed its cloak of words; and Truth, to be accepted, needs but to be revealed clearly, for Truth is its own
defense and its own proof.[101] Therein lies the reason for our
hope that the New Method may serve to acquaint barbarous
nations not only with our languages and our customs but
also with our creed. Indeed, the highest aim of the New
Method is to promote the study of the Gospel, because the
Gospel offers salvation to all nations and brings to primitive
peoples a knowledge of the highest good, which is God. Like
William Bathe's Irish *Ianua*, which, according to Scioppius,
was especially designed to propagate the faith among the
Indians of America, our work is intended not only to
facilitate the study of languages but also to provide a better
means for teaching Christianity to the heathen.[102] [This
chapter concludes the discussion of the New Method as an
educational system. The last three chapters of the book
exhort scholars, theologians, and secular authorities to
sanction and support the New Method in so far as it makes
any valuable contribution to the advancement of learning.]

Chapter xxviii.—An appeal to the judgment of learned
men. The author asks scholars to evaluate the usefulness of

100. Again Comenius foreshadows the conjectures of modern semantics;
his views, however, are very temperate; he believes that words aggravate
misunderstanding but do not cause it.

101. These Platonic assumptions underlie the whole system of Comenian
scientific, philosophical, educational, and irenic speculation.

102. For the Irish *Ianua* see chap. viii above, pp. 51–52; for Comenius'
interest in the education of American Indians see the end of chap. xxviii
below.

the New Method. He regrets the prolixity and the deficiencies of this work but regards the method as public property and therefore urges the learned to point out faults and to suggest improvements. Since the method is intended for practical use, he hopes that teachers will not judge it in the vacuum of speculation but will put it to the test of practice. The author is aware of the incompleteness of the present work; he accomplished what he could, not what he would. Therefore, he asks for something more than criticism; he beseeches learned men to assist him in supplementing this work, which is only a tentative effort many parasangs removed from the completeness desired. The method should be extended to other languages than Latin and also to the study of the arts, philosophy, medicine, and theology; for we can hope for no thoroughgoing reform of our schools unless we are supplied with systematic and reliable surveys of these subjects. The author himself intends to follow the present work with a *Ianua rerum*, which will outline an improved method for the study of *realia*.[103] He invites other scholars to collaborate with him in producing an encyclopedia of all knowledge.

The author also begs the learned men of all nations not to hold the vernacular in contempt but to cherish it and develop its resources. Every highly civilized language was once rude speech that achieved elegance only because native

103. This work appeared posthumously as *Ianua rerum reserata, hoc est sapientia prima (quam vulgo metaphysicam vocant), etc.* (Leyden, 1681); it was printed by the house of Jacob Heeneman and probably edited by Christian V. Nigrin. See Novák-Hendrich (p. 672) for evidence that the work was completed by 1670 and that parts of it were printed under the author's supervision. It is not a scientific treatise in the modern sense of the word but an outline of Comenian psychology, epistemology, and metaphysics; it deals not with things as they are but as they presumably have existed from all eternity in the form of ideas or exemplars. By co-ordinating science and religion in a universal parallelism, Comenius attempts to construct a dialectical basis for pansophy.

writers cultivated it and gave it polish. We remember Cicero not because he excelled in foreign speech but because he helped to refine his native Latin. Petrarch and Bembo, despite their undeniable mastery of Latin, are illustrious because they added grace to their native Italian. It is reprehensible to neglect the vernacular, but it is shameful to be learned in foreign tongues yet ignorant of the structure and the history of one's native speech. As chapters v and xxi of the present work make clear, the New Method can be adapted to instruction in the vernacular. For the twenty-odd languages of Europe scholars could prepare vestibular, ianual, and atrial textbooks, so that our civilization might be enriched by the cultivation of all European languages.

Another way of cultivating native speech is to found academies like the Florentine society of La Crusca[104] or the German Societas Frugifera (Die Fruchtbringende Gesellschaft)[105] founded in 1617 under the auspices of the prince of Anhalt. Such academies would make an extensive examination of the historical and linguistic antiquities of their nation; they would reduce the vernacular to grammatical rules and thereby lay a foundation for an inquiry into its nature and its special characteristics; they would also make a systematic study of all the sounds, phrases, and idioms of

104. Accademia della Crusca ("academy of the bran"); its emblem was a sieve, and its object was to sift and purify the Italian language. It was founded in 1582 and based the first edition of its dictionary, *Vocabulario della Crusca* (Venice, 1612), on strictly Tuscan usage.

105. This "fruitful" society was also known as the Palmenorden; its symbol was a palm with the inscription "Alles zum Nutzen." Each member had a quaint title and as his personal emblem a plant or vegetable. Prince Louis of Anhalt was called "The Nourisher" (*Der Nährende*), and his emblem was wheat bread. Among the illustrious members were the dukes of Weimar and of Brunswick; five princes were among the original members. The seat of this academy was first Cöthen, then Weimar, and finally Halle. See Reber, p. 512.

native speech in order to compile accurate dictionaries and dependable lexicons.

Work on individual languages must be supplemented by polyglot studies, because without an insight into the nature of other languages we cannot properly understand the structure of our own speech. Even the learned Harsdörffer arrives at some absurd etymologies in Germanic merely because of his faulty knowledge of Slavic.[106] To extend our knowledge of linguistic similarities and differences, a philological society (*collegium philologicum*) should undertake a co-operative project in which scholars could vie with one another and at the same time collaborate in producing vestibular, ianual, and atrial texts for all the European languages. In time the work might be extended to include Asiatic, African, and American languages, a task which presents no insurmountable difficulties, because the Europeans who have dealings with alien peoples could introduce them to our methods of language-teaching. We firmly believe that among these barbarian nations many a gifted youth, if properly trained in Latin and in the principles of studying languages by the parallel method, could become, like another Cadmus, the founder of his nation's letters. The author has a special interest in such undertakings because they may help to spread Christianity among American Indians.[107] He has been profoundly moved by the vast possibilities suggested in Johannes Laet's description of America as a land remarkable

106. The reference is to pars. 5–8 of "Disquisitio I" in *Specimen philologiae Germanicae* (Nuremberg, 1646). George Philip Harsdörffer (1607–58) was one of the founders of the Societas Florigera or Blumenorden, organized on the model of the Palmenorden. The Blumenorden began meeting in 1644 in Nuremberg, where it survived into the twentieth century. Comenius corresponded with Harsdörffer (see Josef Reber, *I. A. Comenius und seine Beziehungen zu den Sprachgesellschaften* [Leipzig, 1895]).

107. See R. F. Young, *Comenius and the Indians of New England* (London, 1929).

for its diversity of speech, a land where the languages are as numerous as the tribes, and the tribes are innumerable.[108]

Chapter xxix.—A digression addressed to theologians. The author urges religious scholars not to obstruct but to aid these studies because training in languages is a necessary preparation for the preaching of the gospel and because schools are the seminaries of the church in the sense that a congregation is as receptive to instruction as schools have made it. Furthermore, our didactic and pansophic efforts in no way usurp the place of religion, nor do they breed contempt for piety. The author is not trying to further the dark purposes of some strange cult; his subject is the common nature of things, the common light of truth, and the common sense innate in each of us.[109] Nor is the author promoting the cause of any particular sect; he wishes to share with all mankind whatever wisdom he may possess and to alleviate the burdens of all his fellow-men. Because he is willing to learn as well as to teach, he has sought the guidance of illustrious scholars. Ratke, it is true, made no reply, but others commended the work; among these, J. V. Andreae was especially encouraging and carried on an extensive correspondence with the author. [Excerpts from Andreae's letters follow.][110] The theologians may rest secure that the author seeks no

108. The reference is to *Notae ad dissertationem Hugonis Grotii de origine gentium Americanarum.* Johannes de Laet of Antwerp (*ca.* 1586–1649), director of the West Indies Company, was a famous geographer and cartographer; he designed a series of excellent maps for the Elzevir press and was the author of several historico-geographical works, among them *Novus Orbis sive descriptionis Indiae occidentalis libri xviii* and *Historia naturalis Brasiliae.* Cf. Reber, p. 515.

109. "Common sense" in earlier usage means the mental ability to unify the impressions conveyed by the five physical senses.

110. For Andreae see especially Ludwig Keller, "Johann Valentin Andreae und Comenius," *MCG*, XI (1892), 229 ff., and Max A. H. Möhrke, *Johann Amos Komenius und Johann Valentin Andreae, ihre Pädagogik und ihr Verhältniss zu einander* (Leipzig, 1904).

useless quarrels; his sole purpose is to provide Christian youth with an agreeable method of instruction.

Chapter xxx.—An appeal to secular authorities. The governors of nations, being sacredly bound to guard the well-being of the people, should see to it that the light of true knowledge shines throughout the land. They must therefore use their power to establish and to maintain properly organized and well-equipped schools which will serve the people's welfare.

To explain briefly the purpose of the present work, let us consider the ancient fable of the labyrinth which relates how Theseus escaped from his hopeless prison only with the help of Ariadne's thread. Even such a labyrinth is the perplexed and confused life of man, a labyrinth from which none can escape unless he possess the true thread of Ariadne, the Creed.[111] Wherever we turn, we discover a labyrinth. Each

111. Cf. Ovid *Heroides* x. During the Renaissance classical legends were commonly allegorized for religious, ethical, and even scientific purposes. Reber (p. 522) believes that here Comenius was especially influenced by *De augmentis*, Book ii, chap. 13, where Bacon illustrates the uses of parabolic poesy by making Pan, Perseus, and Dionysus the symbols of things natural, political, and moral. A more immediate source, I believe, is Bacon's own use of the phrase *filum labyrinthi* to describe his inductive method of "inquiry and practice" (cf. *Novum organum*, Book ii, chap. 50). Bacon entitled three of his shorter works *Filum labyrinthi;* these appear in Spedding's edition of Bacon's *Works* as *Filum labyrinthi* (ii, 687–89); *Filum labyrinthi, sive formula inquisitionis* (ii, 496–504); and *Filum labyrinthi; sive inquisitio legitima de motu* (iii, 625–40). One of Comenius' most popular works and a classic of Czech poetic prose is entitled *Labyrint světa a lusthaus (ráj) srdce* ("The Labyrinth of the World and the Paradise of the Heart"). This satirico-mystical allegory, the Preface of which is dated 1623, relates how a Pilgrim in his wanderings through the mazes of this world discovers in all the estates and conditions of men only fraud, deceit, error, and confusion. The first part of the work is a realistic picture of seventeenth-century society at almost all levels; especially notable is the vivid portrayal of the quackery of alchemists and Rosicrucians, the chicanery of university officials, the narrow-mindedness of sectarians, and the brutality and venality of the military and knightly orders. The work has been translated into English by Count Lützow (New York, 1901) and by Matthew Spinka (Chicago, 1942).

man is unto himself an endless labyrinth of sensation, desire, reasoning, and striving. Our very schools are a labyrinth in which youth struggles to escape from ignorance, for each science, art, and language is a labyrinth of perplexities. No one can find his way through our present-day maze of courses, books, and libraries unaided. To escape from blind error and confusion, one must be guided by a thread that will stretch through all the reaches of learning and will prove simple, uniform, and ready for use. Such a thread the author has tried to fashion in the New Method. He now respectfully submits the work to the arbiters of the world's affairs and awaits their verdict, begging them to appraise the value of his undertaking and to judge whether he has achieved a useful result. His aim throughout has been to facilitate the study of language in order to facilitate the study of things and, by instilling a better, truer, and fuller knowledge of things, to imbue the minds of the young with a little more wisdom.

Since the chief purpose of this first edition is to offer the work for criticism and correction, the author hopes that the secular authorities will deign to submit the New Method to the judgment of those who are capable of judging its worth and of deciding whether it contains any admixture of harmful error.

At this time the author presumes to remind the governors of the people that they themselves can help to bring about the conditions necessary to the growth of culture. In the name of all the Muses, who never consort with Mars, he entreats the masters of the world's affairs to restore peace in their realms, for peace is the nourisher of felicity. He prays that the age of destructive war may be succeeded by an age of creative peace and that the schools destroyed by devastating wars may be replaced by schools founded on new and better principles. He also implores all rulers to set an example to the learned and the unlearned by cherishing and cultivating the vernacular. Such an example was set by heroic figures in times past. Charlemagne introduced a higher culture among his people and laid the foundations for cultivating the vernacular by cleansing Germanic speech of its barbarous rudeness. Among modern kings James of England merits praise because he charged his son and heir apparent with the duty of cultivating the vernacular and enjoined him to remember that nothing befits a king more than to refine and to enrich the language of his own people.[112]

The author also entreats the civil authorities to aid in the founding of scientific societies and philological academies, especially those which cultivate the national language. Such institutions of learning bring enduring benefits and great honor to a nation, but they require the co-operation of many learned specialists and wide public support. The great Verulam has clearly shown what large advantages are to be derived from such learned societies and why the scholars of a nation should be supported by public funds.[113]

112. A free rendition of an excerpt from the third book of King James's *Basilikòn dôron sive de institutione principis ad Henricum filium*. Literally translated, the passage reads: "To polish and embellish one's own language is not alien to royal dignity." Prince Henry died in 1612. The *Basilikòn dôron*, published four years before James VI of Scotland became James I of England, gives clear evidence that its author was well acquainted with Joachim du Bellay's *La Deffence et illustration de la langue françoyse* (1549), the famous manifesto of the Pléiade which advocates the embellishment (*illustration*) of the vernacular.

113. At this point Comenius quotes excerpts from Bacon's Preface to the second book of *De augmentis*, pars. 9, 10; the passage, as translated in Spedding, IV, 286–88, reads thus:

"For it is very necessary to the progression of sciences that lecturers in every sort be of the most able and sufficient men; as those who are ordained not for transitory use, but for keeping up the race and succession of knowledge from age to age. This cannot be, except their condition and endowment be

All educational establishments, from the higher institutions to the lowest grades, are of paramount concern to the civil authorities, because the welfare of a nation depends upon the quality of the citizens that its schools produce. Most commendable are the words of Luther when he exhorts the civil powers to establish schools for both sexes throughout the land and urges that every golden coin spent on buildings and fortifications should be multiplied a hundred times to educate a single youth who could be an example and a guide to his fellows. A good and wise man, in Luther's opinion, is the most precious treasure of a commonwealth.[114]

[The work ends with a humble prayer for divine guidance.]

---

such that the most eminent professors may be well contented and willing to spend their whole life in that function and attendance, without caring for practice.

"In general, it may be held for certain that there will hardly be any great progress in the unravelling and unlocking of the secrets of nature, except there be a full allowance for expenses about experiments; whether they be experiments appertaining to Vulcan or Daedalus (that is, the furnace or engine), or any other kind. And therefore as secretaries and emissaries of princes are allowed to bring in bills of expenses for their diligence in exploring and unravelling plots and civil secrets, so the searchers and spies of nature must have their expenses paid, or else you will never be well informed of a great number of things most worthy to be known. For if Alexander made such a liberal assignation of money to Aristotle, to support hunters, fowlers, fishers and the like, that he might be better furnished for compiling a History of Animals; certainly much more do they deserve it, who instead of wandering in the forests of nature, make their way through the labyrinths of arts."

114. Comenius is loosely paraphrasing a passage from the letter entitled *An die Radherrn aller stedte deutsches Lands, das sie Christliche schulen auffrichten und hallten sollen* (1524), which Comenius dates 1525. In this famous address to the magistrates of German cities, Luther urges that schools be established and maintained by the civil powers, not by the church.

THE *ANALYTICAL DIDACTIC*

THE TWO VERSIONS OF THE
ANALYTICAL DIDACTIC

In the translation that follows significant departures of the second edition of the *Methodus* from the text of the first edition are indicated in footnotes. The tenth chapter of the *Methodus* (the *Analytical Didactic*) is introduced differently in the two editions which Comenius himself published.

LESZNO EDITION (1648/9)
CHAPTER X

The didactic art as a foundation for the newest method of teaching languages. General matters are treated from Section 1 to 39, special topics to Section 127, and, finally, very special topics (concerning rapid, agreeable, and thorough methods of teaching) from Section 128 to the end.

AMSTERDAM EDITION (1657)
CHAPTER X

The didactic art as a foundation for the newest method of teaching languages consists of three parts:

I. The End that it seeks to achieve: to teach rapidly, agreeably, and thoroughly (1–4).
II. The Means by which it strives to attain this objective; these are either constant, that is, examples, precepts, imitation, and their proper uses (5–38), or varied and employed according to the variety of
   1. the subjects to be learned (39–106 [*sic*]);
   2. the persons to be instructed (110–23);
   3. the ends to be attained (124–28).
III. Certain concise methods for teaching all subjects rapidly (129–40), agreeably (140–49), and also thoroughly (150–62 [*sic*]).

I

GENERAL DIDACTICS

1. Didactics is the art of good teaching. (In Greek *didásko* means "I teach"; *didaktós*, "one who has been taught"; *didaktikós*, "apt at teaching," that is, "one who knows how to teach.")

2. To teach is to enable someone else to learn and know what you know.

3. To teach well is to enable someone to learn rapidly, agreeably, and thoroughly.

Rapidly: with one uninterrupted endeavor, without any harmful loss of time. Agreeably: in the whole course of any study a pupil should feel not so much wearied by what he has performed but rather inspired by a desire for what remains to be accomplished. Thoroughly: what he learns he should learn completely and correctly, so that he can readily put it to use. It follows that he who imparts knowledge slowly, tiresomely, and incompletely teaches badly.

4. To teach skilfully is to know reliable methods of good teaching and to adhere to them, so as to promote knowledge of things rapidly, agreeably, and thoroughly.

In teaching and in learning speed is necessary, because art is long and life is short, etc. Pleasure is necessary, because it prevents those plagues of instruction, boredom and disgust, from creeping in and because it stimulates the mind and keeps it interested in the work. Thoroughness is necessary, so that our knowledge may be real knowledge and not a shadow of knowledge, a reality and not an illusion; otherwise we may deceive ourselves or others. In each and every respect art is necessary, because art is a sure method of performing anything surely.

To teach or learn or work without sureness betrays lack of skill.

5. Therefore, we shall explore these paths of the art of teaching and examine all the general and particular activities that meet in the act of teaching, learning, and knowing, to the end that we may determine what their nature is, what they consist of, and how they develop, for in that way we may determine how we can, wish, and ought to treat them. A proper investigation of these general activities will yield rules for prudent teaching, rules of general application and lasting validity, which must be observed always and everywhere, whereas an investigation of special activities will yield special rules, which are to be observed only in some situations and on some occasions.

6. Always and everywhere in the act of teaching and learning these same activities come together: to teach, to learn, to know. Therefore, we must first of all probe these activities to the core, so that the requirements of each may be perfectly clear. Since the act of knowing precedes the act of teaching (for no one can teach what he does not know), let us first inquire into this act of knowing.

7. To know is to be able to represent something by means of thought, deed, or word.

For all things come to us by way of representation or imagination, that is, through the fashioning of copies and images of things. Indeed, whenever I perceive anything with my senses, its image is imprinted on my brain. Whenever I produce its likeness, I imprint its image on matter. Finally, when my tongue declares what my mind or hand is shaping, it imprints the image of that thing upon the air and thereby into the ears, brain, and mind of another person. (See II, 20.)[1] To represent anything

1. A reference to the second chapter of the *Linguarum methodus novissima:* "It is well known that speech cannot exist without some external signs, because all speech, as well as all thought and action, comes into being through images. Indeed, God the Creator first conceived images, forms, and ideas and then impressed them upon things. Things, in turn, impressed

in the first way is *to know* (German *wissen*, Čech *věděti*); to be able to represent anything in the second and third ways is *to know how* (German *können*, Čech *uměti*).

8. Therefore, wherever we find knowledge, there we find three components: an idea, an expression of that idea, and an expresser of that idea; that is, (1) an archetype or original image, which is the object of knowledge; (2) an ectype or representation of that image, which is the result of knowledge; and (3) some instrument which transforms the first into the second, for example, the senses, the hand, the tongue, etc. (For without an instrument nothing can be produced.) Deprive the mind of the objects from which it derives images or of the instrument (the senses, the hand, the tongue) by which it gives them form, and the mind will be unable to create an image of anything; that is, it will be unable to know (think, produce, utter) anything. Deprive the mind of the images that it has fashioned (as happens with loss of memory, when images in the brain are obliterated), and the mind will no longer know anything. From this begin to emerge certain axioms:

I. *There is no knowledge without an idea or original image.*
   Or, knowledge is a knowledge of something. Therefore, if you are to know anything, you must find something to which you can adapt your senses and through them your

---

their likenesses upon the senses, the senses upon the mind, the mind upon the tongue, and the tongue upon the air and the ears. When the mind is impregnated with concepts of things and wishes in turn to imprint its images upon another mind, it must represent those images by means of some external representations upon the senses of another person and thus transmit the images to the mind of that person, because, as long as our minds are inclosed in bodies, no two minds have direct contact with each other, nor can they reveal their concepts to each other without intermediaries (as we believe angels can do)."

mind, hand, and tongue. Knowledge and skill must have a model.[2]

II. *There is no knowledge except through the transformation of ideas into images.*

Or, knowledge is image-making. Knowledge and skill subsist in imitation.[3]

III. *There is no knowledge without an instrument of representation or means of image-making.*

For knowledge represents something by means of something else. Knowledge and skill must possess creative means.[4]

9. To learn is to proceed to a knowledge of something unknown by way of something known.

Or, to learn is to endeavor to represent something by means of images.

10. Therefore, whenever we learn something, three things are present: (1) something unknown toward which we strive; (2) something known through which it is possible to arrive at the unknown; and (3) an attempt to make the transition and thereby the transition itself. The process of learning, *discentia* (a word used by Tertullian for the act of learning),[5] is a sort of motion whereby a movable object is advanced from a given landmark upon which it rests to another landmark some distance away. This movable object is the pupil. The first landmark is something which the pupil already

2. Comenius writes this sentence in German: "Wissenschaft und Kunst muss Vorbild haben." For the development of this notion, later popularized by John Locke, see Secs. 28 and 53 below.

3. Comenius writes this sentence in German: "Wissenschaft und Kunst bestehet im Nachbilden."

4. This sentence is also in German: "Wissenschaft und Kunst muss Bildungsmittel haben."

5. *De anima* 23 and 24. In par. 15 of "Greeting to the Reader" in the *Magna*, where Tertullian is also cited, Comenius uses the word *discentia* for the art of teaching. In the posthumous *Spicilegium didacticum* (Amsterdam, 1680), he uses the word *mathetica* for the art of learning.

knows and by which he can profit in advancing to a knowledge of the second, hitherto unknown landmark. (This we call preliminary knowledge or the beginning of knowledge.) From here we proceed to the distant landmark, the thing unknown, but not without a certain effort. For example, if today I have to learn the Persian language, I am confronted by an unknown subject. In order to learn it, I require aid from the known, say, an interpreter acquainted with both that language and mine (either a living interpreter—a human being; or a lifeless one—a dictionary). Finally, I have need of industry and zeal, so that by successive interpretations and by frequent repetition I may gain knowledge of a hitherto unknown language through the aid of a language I already know. Omit any one of these ingredients, and learning will come to naught.

Hence the following axioms:

IV. *We do not learn what we already know.*

Because it is already known; to do something already done is neither necessary nor possible.

Corollary: Therefore, whatever we learn, while we are learning it, is unknown. One ceases to learn what one has already learned.

V. *We learn the unknown only through the known.*

Or, whatever we learn, we learn through what we knew before, because no other course is possible. Knowledge of things comes in successive steps, and human understanding is a sort of upward climb to that which we seek. Therefore, just as there are steps on a ladder and he who climbs the ladder does so in no other way than by advancing from the step on which he stands to the next step (should he attempt to do otherwise, he would experience a fall), so, in the process of learning, the mind advances in no other way than from one step to the next, from the already known to that which is still to be known.

Corollary: Therefore, we do not learn the unknown through another unknown.

VI. *We learn the unknown only by learning.*

Or, we must learn that which we would know.

Corollary: Therefore learning requires industry, diligence, etc.

11. He who travels any road for the first time must be careful not to lose his way, and he who tries to climb a ladder for the first time must take care not to miss the steps, for rarely is a man so cautious that he may not chance to stray. That is why it is very useful, necessary indeed, to have a guide who will prevent you from straying and call you back if you do stray, a guide who will keep you on the steps and lift you if you fall. The same conditions exist in the process of learning, where the mind advances from the known to the unknown; hence the following axioms:

VII. *A student must always beware of learning anything badly.*

VIII. *Even a cautious student finds it impossible to avoid error at first.*

Or, we learn nothing without making some mistakes.

IX. *A student can become proficient only by degrees.*

X. *Therefore, a student always needs someone to guide him, admonish him, and correct him.*

Of course there are some exceptionally gifted natures that stimulate, admonish, guide, correct, and reprove themselves, but they are rare. And even they are not without guidance, advice, and correction, since they provide for themselves what others must get from their fellow-men. Ordinary natures, to say nothing of slow ones, always need a guide.

Corollary: He who teaches, guides; he who learns is guided.

Let us then proceed to determine what is required of the teacher in his capacity as a guide.

12. To teach means to introduce the student to instruction. Here we have teacher, student, and instruction! The teacher is he who imparts knowledge, the student is he who receives it, and instruction is the act of imparting knowledge

—a transfer from teacher to student. (Section 17 and the following.)

XI. *Where no one teaches, nothing is taught.*

XII. *Where no one learns, nothing is learned.*

XIII. *Where there is no instruction, there is no transplanting of knowledge.*

13. Indeed, the same conditions are required for the development of talent as for the development of farmland, for the growth of instruction as for the growth of a seed. If you sow nothing, you will reap nothing; if you sow little, you will reap little. Nor will you reap anything but what you sow, because talent, like a croft, gives back nothing but what it has received.

XIV. *Teacher and student are complemental; neither can be absent from the act of teaching.*

XV. *The bond between teacher and student is instruction, as it passes from one to the other.*

XVI. *A good teacher, a good student, and good instruction increase knowledge mightily.*

Let us then see what are the good qualities required of each.

14. A teacher should have the ability to teach; that is, he should possess knowledge and also have the skill and the desire to teach. In other words, (1) he himself should know that which he is to teach to others (for no one can teach what he knows imperfectly); (2) he should be able to teach others what he himself knows (that is, he should be a capable teacher, one who knows how to bear the ignorance of his students patiently and also how to dispel that ignorance effectively); finally, (3) he should also desire to teach what he knows and what he can teach (that is, he should be industrious and diligent as well as eager to guide others into the light in which he himself rejoices).

XVII. *A teacher should be competent to teach (a learned teacher).*

XVIII. *A teacher should be skilful in teaching (a capable teacher).*

XIX. *A teacher should be zealous in teaching (a teacher to whom indolence and distaste are unknown).*

15. The student should be teachable; that is, he should have the ability, knowledge, and desire to be taught. The ability to receive instruction consists in having unimpaired organs for learning (sense, hand, and tongue). The knowledge required consists in being of an age and a development mature enough for the subject of instruction. The desire to be taught consists in craving instruction and drinking it in with eager senses. Therefore,

XX. *You will teach nothing to one who is incapable of being taught.*

> For example, optics to the blind, music to the deaf, speech to the mute, dances to the lame, etc. That is impossible.

XXI. *You will find it difficult to teach one who is unripe for instruction.*

> For example, to teach an infant how to speak grammatically, how to sing according to musical rule, how to employ perspective; also, to teach him how to run before he knows how to walk or how to walk before he can stand on his feet, etc. That would be as though you expected a featherless bird to fly or tried to pluck fruit from a tree hardly in bloom. There is a time for everything. Ripeness, of course, is here to be understood as ripeness not merely of age but also of development, because we learn all things gradually, through a knowledge of their antecedents (according to Axiom V). Unless one knows the step which leads to the next step, he will be unable to advance, except with difficulty.

XXII. *You will teach in vain one who is uninterested, unless you first make him eager for learning.*

> So that he will have a desire for knowledge, bring enthusiasm to the work, lay aside other interests, and attend to the task

in hand. How this is to be brought about we shall indicate presently.

16. Hence there emerge three kinds of teachableness: first, readiness to perceive, or aptitude; second, ability to discriminate, or discernment; third, zeal to push forward a task once begun, or diligence. Apt is he who of his own accord grasps all that he encounters. Discerning is he who understands well what he has pondered well. Diligent is he who masters anything whatsoever through hard work.

XXIII. *Aptitude, discernment, and diligence, if present together, make for remarkable progress.*

XXIV. *Lack of aptitude or discernment must be compensated for by diligence.*

XXV. *Where there is neither aptitude nor discernment nor diligence, teaching and learning prosper little or not at all.*

17. Teaching also consists of three parts: the thing taught, the manner of teaching it, and some means of furthering instruction so that it will be attentively received. The thing taught is called the object of instruction; the manner of teaching it is called method; the means of furthering instruction is called discipline. Thus the word *discipline* is, as it were, a *discipellina* because by discipline an unwilling pupil is driven (im*pelli*tur) to learning (ad *disc*endum).

XXVI. *Where nothing is taught, there nothing is learned.*

XXVII. *Where teaching is confused, there learning is confused.*

XXVIII. *Where teaching is careless, there learning is careless.*

Corollaries: 1. Multiplicity of knowledge depends upon multiplicity of objects studied.

2. Orderliness of knowledge depends upon orderliness of instruction.

3. Progress in knowledge depends upon the diligence of teachers and students.

18. The proper subjects of instruction are all those matters which cultivate and perfect human nature; that is, a knowl-

edge of ourselves and thereby the ability to use our own limbs, senses, mind, will, etc., and also a knowledge and ability to use what is around us, so that all things may serve us and none may harm us. What these various matters are we shall see later, when we have occasion to inquire into the particular laws of teaching.

19. The manner of teaching is provided by method, which the teacher should adhere to always and everywhere, so that he will know how to make the minds of students teachable (see Sec. 20), how to impart instruction (see Sec. 26), and how to fasten this instruction in the mind that has received it (see Sec. 34). A painter who is about to create a portrait first stretches the canvas or smooths the board on which he intends to paint and covers it with some foundation, so that it will be ready to receive the pigment. Only then does he paint. Finally, he covers the painting with varnish and exposes it to sun and air, so that it will harden and become safe to handle. He who sets about the task of implanting knowledge and skill into the mind, hand, and tongue of another will follow the same wise procedure if he knows how to prepare minds for instruction, how to impart that instruction, and, finally, how to make it stick fast.

20. He who is about to learn needs preparation, so that he will be able, will desire, and will know how to receive instruction. For if he is unable, is unwilling, and does not know how to receive it, you will only weary yourself and him with futile and burdensome instruction, as is clear from Section 15. Therefore, consider this as a law:

XXIX. *Do not undertake to teach one who is not ready to be taught.*

It is pointless to speak to one who will not hear, to show anything to one who will not look, to lead one who will not follow. That is why we do not teach one who is not ready to learn. If you persist in such a task, you will lose time and trouble. (See Axioms XX, XXI, and XXII.)

21. To be able, to be willing, and to know how to receive instruction are qualifications which come to us naturally or must be deliberately acquired. If nature endows a person with healthy organs, zeal for learning, and the perseverance to accomplish things (sometimes more fortunate natures are so endowed), it would be a mistake to delay him with preliminaries. Let him set to work. There is no need to commend food to a hungry man; merely offer it to him, and he will seize it greedily and digest it thoroughly. Therefore,

XXX. *Do not postpone the instruction of one who is ready to receive it.*

22. If, however, the stomach feels distaste for food, you may be sure that it needs medicine before nourishment; therefore, put aside the food and provide medicine. If anyone harbors a distaste for instruction, it is because he does not understand its usefulness, because he is attracted more by something else, or because he is frightened by difficulties. Therefore, make him understand how it is to his advantage to know a particular subject, and he will readily desire to know it, because the love of better things is innate in the human mind. Give him a taste of something good, and you will observe how quickly he is attracted, because it is natural to pursue goodness of any sort. Make him feel that the difficulties are not insuperable, and he will hasten to undertake the task, because the desire to be active and to seek mastery over things is characteristic of the human mind.

XXXI. *Do not undertake to give instruction unless it commends itself to the pupil.*

Corollary: Therefore you must strive in every possible way to make the pupil regard his task as something worthy of admiration.

This admiration will arouse love, love will arouse desire, and desire will arouse diligence.

23. You will bring about this condition if you give him an example of the excellence, agreeableness, and facility of the study he is beginning; for it is natural to prefer the whole to the part. The truth of this observation you can test on any child of three, four, or five years. Begin to relate to him a tale or fable and, after beginning, stop. How he will fret to know the rest; how he will beg you to continue! This is true of all situations, no matter what the age of the person, provided we know how to make use of natural incentives. Therefore,

XXXII. *Do not undertake to instruct a pupil unless his appetite has been keenly whetted.*

24. Furthermore, human nature delights in activity and forward movement, especially unhampered movement, whereby it can create things and transform them at will; therefore,

XXXIII. *Do not undertake instruction unless the pupil is equipped for the task.*

Not very sound is the rule given to us recently by certain educators:[6] "All the work should fall to the lot of the teacher; nothing but Pythagorean silence remains for the student." (Chap. viii, Sec. 16.)[7] Such advice urges upon teachers

6. Wolfgang Ratke (Ratichius of Holstein) (1571–1635), reformer of schools in Cöthen, and his adherents.

7. This is a reference to an earlier passage in the *Linguarum methodus novissima:* "vult praeceptorem solum agere omnia, discipulis silentium iniungit Pythagoricum." There, as here, Comenius assails the theories of Ratke. Reber's note on the earlier passage (p. 288) presents evidence that Comenius was acquainted with two of Ratke's works: (1) the Leipzig edition of the essay *In methodum linguarum generalia*, first published in Halle (1615) under the title *Desiderata methodus nova Ratichiana linguas compendiose et artificiose discendi*, and (2) "Artickel, auf welchem führnehmlich die Ratichianische Lehrkunst beruhet" in the *Methodus institutionis quadruplex* (Leipzig, 1617). Of the twenty-five *Artickeln*, Comenius has especially in

ineffectual and useless labor, drudgery fit for a donkey; it sets up unavoidable obstacles to a student's progress and benumbs his attention completely. In Axiom VI and its corollary we saw that learning requires hard work, and in Axiom XIV we learned that in the act of teaching neither teacher nor pupil must be found wanting. That is, each must do his part of the work, the teacher leading the way and the pupil following. If the pupil is to be merely silent, you will not succeed in making him attentive, much less proficient, even though you wear yourself to tatters. Indeed, the more you force him to listen in silence, the more you deaden his interest. For man is not a block of wood from which you carve a statue which is completely subject to your will; he is a living image, shaping, misshaping, and reshaping itself according to opportunity. In fact, even we adults know from experience that nothing is more difficult than to give a teacher undivided attention; much less easy is it for children, whose interests tend to wander. (We shall have occasion to say more about this in Sec. 143 below.) But if you give the pupil something to do, you will quickly rouse and capture his interest, so that he will throw himself into the work. You will note how very natural it is for him who is carried or who rides to pay no attention to the road; but he who must walk unaided looks around carefully so as not to fall or lose his way. Let us, therefore, discard the harmful rule [of Ratke] and substitute a better one:

XXXIV. *The student should work and the teacher should direct.*

In keeping with this rule, always put implements into the hands of a pupil, so that he will realize that he must get things done and so that he will not think of any subject as

---

mind *Artickel* 13: "Alle Arbeit fallet auf den Lehrmeister"; and *Artickel* 14: ". . . dem Lehrjungen gebührt zuzuhören und still zu schweigen. . . . Der Lehrjunge soll nichts reden, in wehrender Lection auch nichts sagen. Denn sonst verhindert er beyde, den Lehrmeister und seine Mittschüler, dass die Lection nicht kan zur rechten Zeit vollendet werden. Hat er aber etwas nöthigs zu fragen, so schreib er beyseit auff, und nach gehaltener Lection hat er zu fragen Zeit genug."

remote, arduous, or difficult. In this way you will quickly make him enthusiastic, spirited, and eager.

25. But how shall we make him capable of being taught? This requires no special art. If you know how to teach, he will know how to receive your instruction (provided he is already eager to be taught). If you know how to lead the way, he will know how to follow, just as an infant is able to suck if the nurse knows how to suckle him. That is why we must take the next step and examine this art of imparting instruction.

26. The highest law and guiding light, the center and circumference, the foundation and summit of the art of teaching, is this alone: Teach everything through examples, precepts, and use or imitation. That is, always place the material of instruction before the student's eyes and explain what you have put before him; as for the student, when he has had the material explained and understands it, let him try to express it in a variety of forms until he can reproduce it perfectly. (This follows from Secs. 8, 9, and 10.) Example is a sort of idea or original image (Axiom I), imitation a sort of image-making (Axiom II), precept a sort of instrument to guide imitation (Axiom III). From this foundation rise the following axioms:

XXXV. *Where there is nothing to imitate (i.e., a model), there is no imitation.*

XXXVI. *Where there is no guidance (i.e., precept), imitation is neither easy nor certain.*

XXXVII. *Where there is no imitation (i.e., use, practice, exercises), guidance for imitation and even models are useless.*

27. Thus, you will note, the whole act of teaching and learning involves examples, precepts, and imitation; these three should be the concern of teacher and student alike. Hence these three axioms:

XXXVIII. *The task of the teacher is to present the model, explain it, and show how to imitate it; the task of the student is to pay attention, comprehend, and imitate.*

For it is our assumption that the teacher is a guide and the student a companion of his guide (according to the corollary to Axiom X). Therefore, the former should lead, that is, show the way, and the latter should follow. A guide and his follower should be together.[8]

XXXIX. *Without examples, precepts, and exercises, nothing is taught or learned unless it be incorrectly.*

The truth of the first part of this statement is clearly illustrated by those who are born deaf; since they hear no one speak, they themselves do not know how to speak. How would they learn? Without a model, they cannot learn (according to Axiom V). Indeed, without an example, man does not even learn to walk like a biped, as for instance that Hessian boy who as an infant was seized by wolves and brought up among them. He could do nothing except what he had learned from the example of wild beasts: run on all fours, howl, and grasp his prey with his fingernails. Finally, in his eighth year, when he was caught and began to move among men, he learned from their example to stand erect, walk like a biped, and soon after that even to speak. But to learn solely from examples without precept is the lot of only the more richly talented. And in truth even such self-taught men (*autodídaktoi* in Greek) do not learn without the help of precept; to be sure, they do not receive instruction from others, but they formulate it for themselves from observation. But no one has ever succeeded and no one will ever succeed in learning anything without practice or exercise.

XL. *All things are taught and learned through examples, precepts, and exercises.*

This is most clearly illustrated in the arts and crafts, where —if the procedure is intelligent—a model is always presented

8. Comenius writes this sentence in German: "Ein Vorgänger und ein Nachgänger müssen beysamen sein."

first; then, if necessary, it is explained; and, finally, it is reproduced by imitation. But the same thing happens in theoretical subjects. For, if you want a person to know something, you first of all present it to his senses, and, if necessary, you explain it. Then, in order to see how well he has understood it, you bid him describe it; this description or repetition is a sort of imitation. Thus also is it with morals: first of all you point to something good, and then you prove that it is good, with the result that your listener himself will approve of it, will embrace it, and will hold to it. For the Creator of all things formed human nature in such a way that each of its component parts turns to its proper objective. Show reason what is true (clearly true), and reason immediately grasps it. Show the will what is good (ostensibly and truly good), and the will immediately accepts it. Show the creative faculty what is possible (manifestly possible), and that faculty immediately performs it. Show, I say, to the human mind a pattern of the true, the good, and the possible, explain it properly, in order to avoid errors of perception, and you will quickly see the mind take on the form of that pattern. This, then, is the only, true, lasting, and best method of teaching and learning— none better will ever be devised.

Corollary: Therefore, if you want a student to learn something, reduce it to an example, explain the underlying idea, and then bid him strive to approximate the example.

28. The most natural order for these three steps is that examples should come first and practice should follow, but precepts should accompany both. This is so because examples provide the stimulus, precepts supply information and guidance, and practice gives strength and substance to knowledge. (That we must proceed in this order is evident from Sec. 19.) Therefore,

XLI. *The exemplar should always come first, the precept should always follow, and imitation should always be insisted upon.*

You will note that the accepted method is to give instruction by means of precepts and then to illustrate the meaning of the rules by examples added later. But the more natural order is that the examples should come first, because, in the first place, examples set the objects of imitation immediately before the eyes, whereas precepts introduce it obliquely and indirectly. Thus in the first instance the object is self-evident; in the second, it is automatically obscured, unless clarified by examples. It stands to reason that what is self-evident should come first and what is revealed only by the aid of the former should follow, in keeping with Axiom V. Second, precepts appeal to the understanding, examples to the senses. Sense impression, however, precedes understanding; indeed, nothing exists in the understanding that was not first in the senses. Therefore, whatever touches the senses should precede, and whatever shapes the understanding should follow. Third, precept is something formal, example something material. But I cannot ascribe shape to matter which I do not yet possess; therefore, I cannot give useful precepts about an object which the student has not yet seen. Fourth, examples illuminate precepts, as all agree; why then should not illumination come first? Surely if we are about to enter a dark cave, we wish to have a torch precede us rather than have it offered to us only after we have penetrated into the darkness. Or, to put it another way, who would wish, as he walks along the streets at night, to have a torch carried behind him? Do we not bid a torch-bearer to precede us and light the way? In these matters artisans are indeed farsighted. None of them lectures his apprentice on the abstract rules of his craft; instead, he sets to work, with the apprentice looking on. Thereupon he puts the tools into the boy's hands and teaches him how to handle them and how to use them in imitation; in this simple way the work itself, as it progresses, supplies further instruction. Already in ancient times Quintilian had noted this when he wrote: "Long and difficult is the road by way of precepts, short and effective by way of examples."[9] Let us therefore correct the common error and let us guide our students to knowledge rather by the short and effective way than by the roundabout and tiresome paths of a long and difficult road. Hence the following

Corollaries: 1. We learn more easily from examples than from precepts.

2. We learn even more easily when the two are combined.

3. But examples should come first.

4. Practice should follow immediately, guided always by appropriate rules.

5. The more examples there are for a single precept, and the fewer the precepts for a multitude of examples, and, finally, the more frequent the use of both, the better.

> A load of rules is a terror, a torment, and a hindrance to the spirit; but the more examples we produce to illustrate a rule already made clear by previous examples, the more does knowledge gain in clarity and certitude. Finally, the more frequent the practice, the more assured the student's knowledge.

29. So much for examples, precepts, and exercises considered together; now let us examine them separately.

30. An example can be presented to a student as something already done or something still to be done. The former method is simpler for the teacher; the latter more useful for the student. An instance of the former you see when a scribe places before a pupil a completed model (*Vorschrifft*) of other people's writing and bids him study it and imitate it. In the second instance the scribe himself writes in the

---

9. Reber notes that Comenius ascribes this passage erroneously to Quintilian; the source is Seneca *Epistle* vi. In this section and also in Secs. 31 and 32, Comenius reveals his modern outlook on education, which meant to him training not only in academic subjects but also in crafts and trades.

presence of the pupil, so that the pupil can observe every movement of hand and pen. The first method is somewhat superficial; the second is more useful. Obviously a pupil is better prepared to imitate if he sees not only what should be done but also how it should be done; this is especially true when he is beginning to learn. (For advanced students, of course, it is not difficult to imitate any finished product.) Therefore,

> XLII. *We can best demonstrate how to do a thing by doing it.* Seneca realized this when he wrote: "We must learn how to do a thing from one who does it."[10] Another writer has said: "To practice an art while another watches is to teach that art." It is better to give no precepts and illustrate by action than to give a multitude of precepts but no demonstration. The eyes indeed are a most trustworthy guide.

31. Actually, however, we do explain examples and give instruction in imitation. Here the teacher must decide whether to use simple and unforced language, as is the custom of artisans, or to employ the precise and formal language of rules, as is customary in the higher disciplines. The two methods, however, can be combined. We may use the simplest possible words in an introductory and general exposition of a subject, but later we usually employ more formal language, when we disclose and explain the set rules that serve to engrave precepts more clearly on the understanding and fix them more deeply in the memory. (As we are doing here in expounding this didactic; at first, when inquiring into the fundamentals of the subject, we employ a certain freedom of expression, then we disclose our findings in more comprehensive terms, and, finally, we compress the results into one or more axioms.) Incidentally, let us call attention to a rule about rules:

10. This idea is expressed in *Epistle* xcviii.—Reber.

XLIII. *The virtue of a rule is that it be brief in words, clear in meaning, and full of truth.*

A rule should be brief, so that it may be easily understood and readily committed to memory. It should be clear, so that it may not suffer from ambiguity. It should be true in all respects, so that it may be subject to the fewest possible exceptions. (Of course in grammar this is not always quite feasible, because of the anomalies of language.) If any material cannot be reduced to a single rule, let us formulate more rules, so as to provide for every exception. That is why in the construction of this didactic we have increased the number of rules rather than weaken rules by exceptions.

32. When we come to the use or application of rules, we again have a choice of two procedures: either to introduce the student to the rules before he undertakes the act of imitation and then leave him to his own resources or to acquaint him with various rules as he encounters new problems. Here we must see to it that the student does not fall into error, and, if he does begin to err, we should immediately stop him short, so that he will not make the same mistake in the future. We must reveal to him the causes of his error, and then, by precept or by rule, we must forestall the danger of new error. The first method is again the simpler for the teacher, but the second is the more profitable for the student. That is, the student will give proper attention to a rule (and its exceptions), will understand it, and will fix it in his memory only when the rule applies as a directive in the actual process of learning (according to Axioms VII and X). In this way and in no other does every craftsman teach the use of rules. Therefore, the following axiom should have the validity of a law:

XLIV. *Rules are more useful if we employ them in conjunction with a task rather than apart from it, because in this way the stu-*

*dent's errors give us an opportunity to repeat the rules and incul-
cate them anew.*

33. Imitation is the task of the student, but the teacher
should ever lead the way, correct faults, and constantly urge
the student to express himself with greater precision (according to the foregoing axiom). Since no one acquires
knowledge except by learning (according to Axiom VI), we
must therefore insist on learning. And since no one learns
anything without making mistakes and errors (according to
Axiom VIII), we must not leave the student to his own
devices; otherwise he will be the more certain to fall into
error (according to Axioms IX and X). Finally, since the
advance from the rudimentary to the perfect is never sudden
(according to Axiom IX), we can insist only on a gradual
progress toward perfection. Therefore,

XLV. *Teacher and student should be mutually attentive.*

XLVI. *The student should follow the teacher at every turn, and
the teacher should ever lead the way.*

XLVII. *Whenever the teacher sees the student deviating into
error, he should admonish and instruct the student to follow in his
footsteps more heedfully.*

Because no one is without error except he who has learned
not to err through frequent error and frequent correction.

34. There are three methods of reinforcing instruction. In
the first place, whatever the subject of study, insist on practice until the student imitates his model with utmost faith-
fulness. Second, introduce fresh material not as if it were
something completely new but as if it were a continuation
of previous endeavor. To that end it is advisable to arrange
the system of every science (and of all other forms of knowledge) into a chain linking all parts. In that way the student
will see how the treatment of later material develops from
earlier studies, is founded upon them, and involves a review

and application of them. Lastly, sprinkle your teaching with constant repetition of earlier matter.

XLVIII. *All parts of instruction should be coherent.*

XLIX. *One topic should not be abandoned for another unless the first has been mastered.*

L. *Later topics should be an occasion for the review of earlier ones.*

> Either theoretically, by means of examination, or practically, by means of exercises; these exercises may be continuous or intermittent and employed as occasion warrants.

35. So much for the manner or method of teaching (beginning with Sec. 19); next comes discipline.

36. In Latin the word *discipline* has several meanings. Sometimes it signifies that which is taught and learned (hence the arts and sciences are called *liberal disciplines*); sometimes it denotes the act of teaching and learning (as when we are said to be brought up under someone's discipline); but the word is used most properly, as here, to denote a means of enforcing instruction. This sort of discipline is always and everywhere necessary if the diffusion of knowledge is to be of any value. Hammer and anvil do not give the right shape to iron if there are no tongs to hold the iron and allow the hammer to strike sure blows; in the same way teacher and teaching fail to give the right stamp to the mind of a pupil if there is no awe or respect to hold his mind in the grip of careful attention.

LI. *Without discipline one learns nothing or at least nothing correctly.*

37. It is desirable, however, to provide a discipline that is adjusted (1) to the end in view; that is, discipline should be efficient in compelling a student to accomplish the task at hand; (2) to human nature; that is, discipline should develop human nature, not destroy it (but since the desire to

be free and unconstrained is inseparable from human nature, which is like an image of God, every forcible discipline seems to be a destroyer of human nature); and (3) to levels of need; that is, just as there are various kinds of talent, so there are various sources and levels of error and the correction of error.

LII. *Discipline should be constant, never slackening; it should always be treated seriously, never in jest.*

LIII. *Discipline should never be harsh.*

LIV. *Discipline should be of various levels.*

38. There are about ten levels of discipline:

(1) A teacher whose learning merits esteem should possess such authority and command such respect that a pupil would think it sinful to offend him.

(2) A teacher should watch his pupils intently, so that they will realize that they are being watched.

(3) A teacher should always lead the way, so that his pupils may see that they have someone to follow.

(4) A teacher should always look about him to see whether he is being followed and how well.

(5) A teacher should constantly lead a pupil by the hand, to make sure that the pupil follows him properly and does not deviate into error.

(6) A teacher should incite his pupils to rivalry (based on friendly competition), so that they may sharpen one another's wits. (Strife enhances virtue.)

(7) A teacher should give frequent tests (sometimes at set intervals, sometimes unexpectedly, especially to the least trustworthy pupils, in order to make sure that they are not missing any part of the instruction).

(8) To make sure that no error becomes a habit, a teacher should always admonish a pupil as soon as the pupil commits a fault (in Axiom XLVII we indicated the force of such immediate correction during the very act).

(9) A teacher should rebuke those who are guilty of wilful error or conspicuous negligence; he should reprimand them and hold them up as a warning example to others, lest impunity become license.

(10) If, however, any pupil should refuse to follow such guidance (although this does not seem possible except in one extremely evil), let him be expelled, lest he prove a hindrance and a stumbling block to others.

Corollaries: 1. We do not want beatings and anger to be part of so sacred a matter as the cultivation of the spirit.

2. If, however, a boy must be whipped, employ the rod rather than the hand and avoid all bitter words, enraged looks, and cruel blows. In that way your pupils will see that you are not indulging in anger and hate but that you are acting advisedly and for their welfare.

39. These general rules of procedure (beginning with Sec. 6) should be observed always and everywhere, whatever the subject of instruction, whether instruction be private or public. Special rules must be evolved from special situations, which do not occur always, everywhere, and in the same way. These special situations are determined by the various objects, subjects, and objectives of instruction, that is to say, the material to be treated (see Sec. 40, etc.), the persons to be educated (see Sec. 110), and the particular aims intended (see Sec. 124).

40. The material to be treated is either good or bad in itself, easy or difficult for us, training the intellect, or the will, or the hand, or even the tongue.

41. Good material is that which is useful to know, and therefore it should be taught: for instance, truth, virtue, skill, speech. Bad material, such as error, fault, blunder, etc., is that which is harmful to learn, and therefore it should be neither taught nor learned; but, if it has crept into the

mind through negligence, we must unteach and unlearn it. On this point let us note the following theorems:

LV. *The bad is learned more easily than the good.*

The reason: The true and good is something single and simple; error has a thousand shapes. Now, it is easier to chance upon one out of a multitude than to discover one that is unique. Hence it is easier to teach wrong things and to teach badly rather than well. Anyone can teach badly; few can teach well.

LVI. *To learn is easier than to unlearn.*

The reason: To learn is to follow nature; to unlearn is to oppose nature. Indeed, our senses instinctively turn toward things and grasp whatever they light upon in their eagerness; when they have once seized upon the likeness of a thing, they are almost unable to relinquish it, because what is once done cannot be undone. What you have not yet seen, you may or may not see in the future; what you have already seen, you cannot erase from your experience.

Hence it is that, whenever you wish to dislodge from your imagination an impression that has been imprinted therein, the more intently and vigorously you struggle to do so, the more deeply you imprint it into the brain. Not without reason did Themistocles[11] wish for the ability to forget rather than for the ability to remember; he judged it to be the misfortune of men that they persist in remembering evil. But let us add that

11. Reber cites Cicero's *De finibus bonorum et malorum* ii. xxxii. 104 and *De oratore* ii. lxxiv. 299; virtually the same story is related in both passages. Simonides, or some other learned man, offered to teach Themistocles the new science of mnemonics. When Themistocles asked what exactly this science could accomplish, he was told that it would enable one to remember everything. According to the *De oratore*, Themistocles replied that the teacher would do him a greater favor "if he taught him to forget what he wanted to forget than if he taught him to remember." The reply in the *De finibus* is, "I should prefer the art of forgetting, for I remember even what I do not want to remember, but I cannot forget what I want to forget."

LVII. *It is (likewise) easier to teach than to unteach.*

The reason: Teaching is a single act: Do thus! Unteaching is a twofold act: Do not do thus, but do thus! Therefore, it was neither a joke nor an injustice when the musician Timotheus[12] exacted a double fee from pupils who had been badly trained in their art, for indeed he had double work with them, first to unteach them what they had learned badly and then to teach them better ways.

42. It follows, then, that we must be specially vigilant that a student learns the good and does not learn the bad, or at least unlearns the bad surely and quickly. Hence these two rules:

LVIII. *Teach nothing that a pupil must unlearn.*

He must unlearn, I insist, by taking pains to rid himself of whatever is wrong, harmful, and offensive, or by discontinuing practices that are unprofitable to life and of themselves later fall into disuse. To burden the mind with such matters is to waste time. Beware of such waste!

LIX. *If a pupil has acquired any wrong knowledge, he should unlearn it as soon as possible.*

For it is better to retreat than to advance in the wrong direction. And we must go back quickly, before error or wrongdoing becomes strengthened by practice and prevents us from retracing our steps. For habit becomes second nature. Hence the poet says: "The mind is slow to unlearn what it spent a long time in learning."[13]

LX. *Since all things are more difficult to unlearn than to learn, we should see to it that there is no need to unlearn anything; we can achieve this in no other way than by taking the precaution not to add bad things to our knowledge or not to learn good things badly.*

12. Reber cites Quintilian *Institutio oratoria* ii. iii. 3: "The task of unteaching is more burdensome than that of teaching. That is why Timotheus, famed for his skill with the flute, is reported to have exacted from those who had been taught by another a fee twice as large as that which was paid by those who came to him without previous instruction."

13. Seneca *Troades* 1. 633: "dediscit animus sero quod didicit diu."

Not only is it "more shameful to drive out a guest than not to let him in,"[14] but it is also more difficult. If, however, we cannot prevent error from intruding, we must unteach it; in Section 123 we shall have occasion to indicate the means of doing so.

43. So much for good and bad subjects; now we must learn the differences among good subjects. Let us begin with the differences that arise when one subject is easier or less easy than another.

44. A thing is easy when it can be accomplished without the extending of one's powers; difficult, if it cannot be so accomplished. Therefore, we learn a thing easily if we learn it without exertion of skill, judgment, or diligence; we learn it with difficulty if we must exert the sinews of our skill, judgment, and diligence.

LXI. *We learn easy things more easily, difficult ones with greater difficulty.*

LXII. *In the mass of subjects to be learned, some are always easier than others.*

LXIII. *Therefore (in the mass of subjects to be learned), we should always begin with the easier and proceed to the more difficult.*

Because the natural powers of the mind (even as the vital power in trees and in our bodies) increase with growth, so that tomorrow you may perhaps be equal to a task to which you are unequal today; and also because God has so ordained all things that the easier things (of the same class) are steps toward the more difficult, just as on a ladder the lower rungs are a means of reaching the higher rungs. We will clarify this presently.

45. Moreover, easier matters actually do come first; that is, (1) the few before the many; (2) the short before the long; (3) the simple before the complex; (4) the general before the particular; (5) the near before the distant; (6) the

14. Ovid *Tristia* v. vi. 13: "turpius eicitur, quam non admittitur hospes."

regular before the irregular, or the analogous before the anomalous.

Surely, (1) you can grasp one thing more easily than two, three, ten, etc.; and (2) you can complete a short journey more easily than a long one. And (3) you can count coins of one kind and value more easily than coins of various kinds. More easily also (4) does a child learn what a tree is and what it is called than he learns to distinguish between pear tree, willow, oak, beech, yew, etc. More easily (5) can you seize something which is at hand than something that you must reach for. Finally, (6) you can more easily come to know a single straight path than one which forks into two, three, four directions. These principles must be regarded as immutable and should have the force of so many precepts, which can be summed up in this single rule:

LXIV. *We must always begin with the few, the brief, the simple, the general, the near, the regular, and proceed gradually to the more numerous, the more extensive, the more complex, the more particular, the more remote, the more irregular.*

Corollary: The comprehension of a later thing presupposes the comprehension of an earlier one.

46. This general rule resolves itself into these particular rules. Let us teach and learn:

LXV. *The few before the many.*

LXVI. *The brief before the long.*

LXVII. *The simple before the complex.*

LXVIII. *The general before the particular.*

LXIX. *The nearer before the more remote.*

LXX. *The regular before the irregular (or the analogous before the anomalous).*

47. Hence it follows that if what we are to teach and learn happens to be slight, short, simple, general, and closely related to knowledge already acquired, we ought to show it to the student, explain it, and assign it for imitation at one

and the same time. (Why break up into several tasks that which can be accomplished with one effort?)

LXXI. *Whatever can be taught and learned in one procedure should never be subdivided.*

48. Contrariwise, whatever is numerous, extended, varied, special, remote, or irregular requires several procedures, as the following rules will indicate.

LXXII. *Whatever is numerous should be gathered into wholes; the larger wholes should be analyzed first, then the smaller ones.*

So that all parts may be classified more easily, observed more clearly, and set in their due places more precisely. Thus simple numbers are gathered into tens, tens into hundreds, hundreds into thousands, etc. Likewise, whoever owns many head of cattle divides them up into flocks and distributes the flocks among various farms, etc.

LXXIII. *Whatever is long should be broken up into well-defined parts, and each part should be taken up in due order.*

Because brief sections, treated one by one, can be covered with greater ease and without tediousness. That is why one breaks a long journey at resting places or inns. But note that, in setting up these divisions, we must consider the following: (1) the natural divisions of the subject; (2) the abilities of the person for whose benefit these divisions are made; (3) finally, the time within which the whole subject, so portioned out, must be covered.

LXXIV. *Whatever is complex should be resolved into its elements, and these should be learned first (in practice they should be performed first).*

This is so because the simple comes before the complex: one before two, two before four, etc.; letters before syllables and words, words before phrases and sentences, etc. And, since it is impossible to combine parts which are not available, we must make sure of each component before we try to construct a whole.

Corollary: To progress from the simple to the complex, from

the complex to the more complex, and from this to the most complex is the art of arts, never and nowhere to be violated.

LXXV. *Individual members should be gathered into kinds, kinds into classes, and classes into a general class. Then, whatever is equally true of all members we may assert about the whole class; on the other hand, whatever differences arise among the various kinds we may indicate for each kind separately, until we come (if need be) to the individual members.*

This is self-evident and needs no illustration.

Corollary: General concepts are the beginning, highly particularized concepts are the perfection, of knowledge.

LXXVI. *Whatever is remote must be approached by steps so carefully chosen that the last step is clearly related to the first by an uninterrupted connection.*

Of course you must guide the student from step to step in orderly fashion, not by fits and starts.

Corollaries: 1. In the treatment of every subject all that follows should be considered as an end; all that precedes, as a means to an end. (In this way all parts will be linked as in a chain.)

2. These steps must not be arranged according to our pleasure but according to the manifest relationships within the subject itself.

Therefore, we must observe these natural divisions scrupulously, so as not to confuse the subject with ourselves.

LXXVII. *Every anomaly should be referred to some analogy by way of subordination.*

That is, every exception should be referred to the rule to which it is an exception.[15] So that nothing may be without its definite place and so that we may more readily perceive why and how anything departs from regularity.

49. So much for the need of beginning with easier subjects and of making more difficult subjects less difficult according to a definite procedure. The following sections provide a special method for training the understanding, the will, the

15. This sentence is found in the Amsterdam edition but not in the Leszno edition.

hand, and the tongue in science, practical wisdom, the arts, and languages (as was proposed in Sec. 40). This distribution of subjects for teaching and learning is derived from the very structure of the human soul. For, in the first place, the soul contains the mind, the mirror of things, which seeks the true; then the will, the critical and selective power, which hungers for the good; third, the executive faculty or power of achieving our desires, which aims at the possible. Finally, added to these, is language, the interpreter, whose function is to extend knowledge, volition, and achievement. And in all these studies uniform guidance is necessary.

LXXVIII. *To know a thing, we must understand it.*

Here, therefore, investigation suffices.

LXXIX. *To esteem a thing, we must understand it and choose it.*

Here, therefore, feelings must also be roused and guided.

LXXX. *To accomplish a thing, we must understand it, choose it, and perform it.*

Here, therefore, in addition to all the preceding, results must be produced.

II

SPECIAL METHODS

A. THE METHOD OF IMPLANTING KNOWLEDGE

50. In common usage *to know* means to perceive a thing historically, that is, to know that it exists; but in philosophical usage the word means to perceive a thing intellectually, that is, to know what it is, whence it derives, and how it came to be.

In the first sense the saying of Augustine is true: "We know many things which we do not understand." In the second sense the saying of the philosopher is true: "To know a thing is to know its causes; that is, to understand it."[1]

51. If we consider only historical knowledge, it is certain that man knows nothing except what he has learned from another, because the soul, inclosed in the dark prison of the body, cannot of itself know anything that happens outside itself, except what is reported by its emissaries, the eyes, the ears, etc.

LXXXI. *No one knows anything (in the historical sense) except what he has learned.*

Therefore: 1. If you want someone to know a thing, acquaint him with it; do not acquaint him with anything you do not want him to know.

2. If you want someone to know many things, see to it that he becomes acquainted with many things.

---

1. Aristotle *Metaphysics* i. i. 17: "It is evident that wisdom consists in the knowledge of certain principles and causes." The distinction between "historical" and "philosophical" knowledge is preserved in the term *natural history* (observation of the phenomena of external nature). Greek *histōr* means "one who knows."

3. If we are industrious and have the opportunity to learn many things, we cannot fail to acquire much knowledge.

52. There are, moreover, three divinely appointed means of learning anything: the senses, reason, and communication. Through the senses we perceive whatever is present. Through reason we infer, from present tokens, whatever is not present to the senses. Through communication we come to know, from another's testimony, whatever is remote (and whatever we have not arrived at by means of the senses or by means of reasoning).

LXXXII. *All our knowledge comes by way of the senses, reason, and communication.*

> There are no other ways by which knowledge of anything can reach us.
>
> Corollary: Therefore, if we are to arrive at a knowledge of things, we must be trained to use our senses, to reason, and to interpret communications about absent things.

53. But because the senses enter into every step of this process (for even reasoning arises from certain tokens perceived by the senses) and because another's testimony about anything can be received only through the senses (notably the sense of hearing), it turns out that, properly speaking, the senses are the only gates through which anything outside of man can find a way to enter the soul; indeed, nothing can enter except in this way. Hence the great truth of the philosopher's statement: "There is nothing in the understanding that was not first in the senses."[2]

2. "Nihil est in intellectu, quod non prius fuerit in sensu"; evidently a rephrasing of Aristotle *De anima* iii. viii. 432a: "No one would ever learn or understand anything if he perceived nothing." This notion, variously interpreted and extended, gains great currency in the seventeenth century, until, of course, it becomes the basic notion of Locke's psychology in the famous passage of Book II, chap. i., par. 2 in *An Essay concerning Human Understanding* (1690). Less than three years after the publication of the Leszno edition of the present work, Hobbes molded the idea into the classic utterance: "... for there is no conception in a man's mind which hath not at

LXXXIII. *The senses are the primary and the constant guides of knowledge.*

Corollary: Therefore, our primary and constant duty is to exercise the senses.

54. The senses grasp the thing itself immediately; reason grasps merely its traces or shadows; communication gives only another's testimony about it. Thus the senses, fixed as they are upon a present thing, give the surest knowledge, whereas reasoning and the testimony of another person are more apt to deceive. Therefore, we say that a man really knows a thing if he perceives it with his senses, that he supposes it if his knowledge depends on reasoning, that he believes it if his knowledge rests on faith in another.

LXXXIV. *The senses are the solid foundations of knowledge.*

Corollaries: 1. Therefore, whenever possible, we should observe[3] everything with our own senses.

2. If anything comes to our knowledge in any other way, we should, if possible, resort to the testimony of the senses, in order to achieve the certainty of truth.

Hence the following: Ocular evidence is the equivalent of proof. We form the best conceptions of things from the things themselves; and, if we have conceived anything differently from what it really is, we can correct the fault by examining the thing itself. For example, anyone who hears a

---

first, totally or by parts, been begotten upon the organs of sense "(*Leviathan* [1651], Part I, chap. i, par. 2). Comenius, however, is discussing here only "historical" knowledge. Throughout his works he asserts his faith in revelation and innate ideas as the sources of "theological" and "philosophical" knowledge.

3. "Ergo omnia propriis sensibus usurpanda...." This anteclassical use of *usurpare* in the sense of "observe, obtain knowledge of" may be an echo of Lucretius *De rerum natura* i. 301, "usurpare oculis," and iv. 975, "sensibus usurpare." Such echoing of phrase proves nothing but does suggest that Comenius may have had in mind the *De rerum*, especially the fourth book, which explains the Epicurean theory of visual images and analyzes the operations and functions of the senses, particularly as they excite the mind and will.

description of an elephant forms some notion of the beast, but rarely a true one. He can form a better one from a picture, but even then he cannot be sure whether his notion is true. What if the painter made a mistake? What if he tried to deceive and deliberately represented some detail otherwise than it really is? But he who has carefully observed a real elephant knows for a certainty what sort of creature it is, and no one can deceive him. Thus we who observe the sun and colors with our own eyes form a true image of them and distinguish them easily, whereas a man blind from birth can hardly do so, even though you describe them to him a thousand times. Hence the saying of Plautus: "Better one eyewitness than ten hearsay witnesses."[4] The same thing is true of the other senses: the object of each sense is the best informant of that sense. Obviously, one is better acquainted with the song of the nightingale, the sweetness of sugar, and the weight of lead if one has heard the song, tasted the sugar, and weighed the lead than if one has merely learned about these matters from hearsay. (See also Axiom CLXIII and its corollary, below.)

55. The more senses anything is impressed upon, the more certainly do we know that thing and the more surely do we retain it.

That is, a person knows better what a bell is if he has seen it, heard it, touched it, and perhaps even rung it than does a person who was born deaf and has only seen it or a person who was born blind and has only heard it.

Hence arises the following axiom:

LXXXV. *We should observe[5] everything with as many senses as possible.*

Through *autopsy* (our own sight), *authapsy* (our own touch), and *autogeusy* (our own taste), etc.: that is, by seeing, touching, tasting, smelling, hearing. Indeed, every facet of an

4. Plautus, *Truculentus*, Act II, scene vi, 1. 7: "Pluris est oculatus testis unus quam auriti decem."
5. "Omnia usurpanda sensibus." See n. 3.

object reveals itself most fully to a different sense, and, therefore, the more senses affected by an object, the fuller our knowledge of that object, as when we come to know wine by its color, its aroma, its taste, etc.

56. Rational knowledge, however, includes the understanding, judgment, and memory. Therefore, let us inquire how we may skilfully guide the mind so that it will properly understand, judge, and remember.

57. To understand is to know the inner structure of a thing which the senses have perceived outwardly. To judge is to appraise the rightness and the fitness of a thing. To remember is to store up for future use the thing we have understood and appraised.

LXXXVI. *We should see to it that whatever has been presented to the senses is also understood.*

Therefore, we should present it in such a way that it can be understood.

LXXXVII. *We should consider whether that which has been understood is right and fitting.*

Therefore, we should present it in such a way that it can be appraised.

LXXXVIII. *We should make sure that whatever has been understood and appraised sticks in the mind permanently.*

Corollaries: 1. Our understanding of anything that the senses have not rightly perceived is worthless. (Therefore, undesirable.)

2. Our judgment of anything that we have not understood is false. (Therefore, undesirable.)

3. Our memory of anything that we have not understood and pondered is fleeting. (Therefore, undesirable.)

58. To understand anything is largely a matter of perceiving why and how that thing in any one of its parts is related to something else and how and to what extent it differs from other things that are similar to it. Indeed, to teach means scarcely anything more than to show how things differ from one another in their different purposes, forms, and origins.

LXXXIX. *To know the differences between things is to know those things.*

Corollary: Therefore, he who differentiates well teaches well.

XC. *To know the causes of things is to know the essence of things.*

Because whatever exists, exists by virtue of its own cause, from which it derives whatever it possesses. Therefore, to teach anything through its causes is to implant it deeply into the understanding.

Corollaries: 1. Therefore, reveal the true end and purpose of each thing.

2. Explain the means that lead to that end; that is, explain the various parts that go to make up the whole form.

3. And also show that the material is capable of taking that form.

4. Finally, show that the thing is capable of giving such form to such material.

If you do this properly, you will find that the student's understanding has been greatly enlightened.

59. And since the understanding of things gives us an internal view of them, it is achieved under the same conditions as an external view. A correct view requires (1) light by means of which the image of anything is detected and carried to the eye; (2) a clear and an open eye which is turned toward the object at the proper distance and receives the image; and (3) sufficient time for the eye to dwell on the object until it has fully examined every part. Similarly, when a subject is presented to the understanding, it cannot fail to be understood if the following conditions are present: (1) clarity of subject matter, either because of the nature of the subject or because of the teacher's exposition; (2) due attention of a sound mind and of the inward eye; and (3) sufficient time for an examination of every part of the subject.

XCI. *We must see to it that what we teach is clearly true.*

Darkness, clouds, and chaos cannot be seen distinctly.

XCII. *We must make sure that what we teach is heeded attentively.*

The brightness of light itself cannot penetrate a closed or an averted eye.

XCIII. *We must take care that what we teach is first understood as a whole, then part by part, each part being distinct and in its place.*

To treat a subject in a casual and perfunctory fashion is to confuse rather than to enlighten the understanding.

60. For a complete view of things we certainly need leisure, so that the eye will not merely glance at them casually but look at them fixedly; for complete understanding of things we also need leisure, so that we may observe each thing with the appropriate sense until we clearly perceive the thing as a whole and all its constituent parts. For almost all things are composite and consist of parts; hence, unless we know all the parts, each one separately, we cannot say that we know the whole. Unquestionably such knowledge of the various parts (one after another) requires time, because human nature is not endowed with the power of concentrating on a variety of matters simultaneously. Make this experiment with your eyes: Can you focus on two things at once? (Even as you read this, can you look at two pages simultaneously, or two lines or words? Indeed, can you look at even two letters in any way but in succession?) Make this experiment with your hearing: Can you be equally attentive to the different utterances of two speakers? Make this experiment with your tongue: Can you distinguish several tastes at one time? Or speak simultaneously in two languages? Or even pronounce two words simultaneously? Make this experiment with your hand: Can you

perform two things at once (e.g., write two letters simultaneously)? You cannot. Objects affecting the same sense get in the way of one another, confuse our perceptions, and thus hinder perception. Nor can our minds be occupied with several lessons at one time. It is certain that, if you perform several things simultaneously, you perform nothing correctly. Therefore,

XCIV. *Attempt only one thing at a time.*

XCV. *Always begin with the whole, then attempt the larger parts, and, finally, the details, one after another.*

XCVI. *Dwell on each part as long as is necessary.*

61. Note carefully that we can and usually do point out, examine, and come to know the parts of anything in three ways: (1) by separating them; (2) by putting them together; and (3) by comparing them with others. For example, you cannot teach anyone how many and what parts go to make up a clock unless you first take the clock apart in his presence, then put the various parts together, and finally compare several clocks and make him see what is peculiar to this or that clock and why this or that part is lacking or appears in a different form elsewhere. Hence it follows that there is a threefold method of explaining and clarifying anything through its component parts: resolution, composition, and comparison or collation, which in Greek we call analysis, synthesis, and syncrisis. To these the following axioms apply with great truth:

XCVII. *We become acquainted with the parts of anything by means of analysis.*

XCVIII. *We come to know them more completely if we also employ synthesis.*

XCIX. *We come to know them most completely if, in addition, we employ syncrisis.*

62. Thus the intellectual method, that is, the way of bringing light to the understanding, is threefold: analytical,

synthetical, syncritical. These modes are properly differ-
entiated in the following way: Analysis begins with the
composite whole (for there is hardly anything so simple that
it does not consist of parts, similar or dissimilar) and ends
with the smallest and simplest particles. Synthesis, on the
other hand, begins with the smallest and the simplest and
ends with the most complex, that is, with the total structure
of each thing. Syncrisis, however, compares wholes with
wholes and parts with parts in parallel fashion. Very true is
the saying, "Parallelism makes for greater clarity."[6]

63. These methods serve the common purpose of making
knowledge clear and distinct, because to make a mental
analysis of a subject is the beginning of understanding, to
put it together again marks an advance in understanding,
and to compare it with all others of the same kind is the
completion of understanding. That is to say, no one knows a
thing perfectly if he knows only that one thing, even though
he knows it both analytically and synthetically; he comes to
understand it fully only when he understands how and why
it resembles other things or differs from them. That is why a
good philologist who is also a polyglot understands languages better than those philologists who know only one
language. Consequently, the syncritic method is a potential
source of much light, because all things are formed, with
minor variations, according to the same exemplars. Whoever pays due regard to this principle is able to see much
that escapes the eyes of others. But this will be discussed
later.

64. Furthermore, the analytic method is useful for discovery, the synthetic for performance, and the syncritic for
both. Certainly, in studying the development of anything,
we necessarily begin by considering its purpose and end, its

6. Comenius writes this saying in Greek: "parállēla phanerótera," lit.,
"parallels [are] clearer."

totality, as it were; then we descend to the conditions and means of its existence, what might be considered its parts; finally, we arrive at the special circumstances of those conditions, its minutest particles, as it were. The synthetic method, however, in the very performance of something, that is, in developing and elaborating it, necessarily begins with the smallest parts and elaborates them as is needed, combining those of equal scope and successively joining larger units with larger, until the composite whole emerges, fully coherent in all its parts. The syncritic method operates in either way, because we can teach subjects by comparing them analytically or synthetically, that is, by showing how things resembling each other can be resolved into their parts or how they can be put together. (In Sec. 59 we discovered the requisites for understanding in the requisites for seeing; in the same way we shall investigate the requisites for judging in Sec. 67 and the following.)

65. This threefold intellectual method can be most aptly compared to the threefold artificial aid to our vision which we call the telescope, the microscope, and the mirror. Just as the telescope brings closer to our vision things far removed, so that they can be examined even in their parts, in like manner does analysis make visible even the hidden parts of anything. And just as the microscope enlarges the smallest of things and reveals even the minutest particles of indivisible units, so synthesis, ever mounting from the lesser to the greater, accurately discloses the precise structure of things. Finally, just as a mirror reflects beams of light and thus brings within our view things placed outside our range of vision, so syncrisis reveals one thing in another under a pleasantly varied aspect. Mirrors, however, are used and always have been used more frequently than telescopes and microscopes. Indeed, the latter are known to few, the former to all; the latter are only recent discoveries, the

former are coeval with the world, being created by God himself, for every body of water and every smooth surface is a mirror. Even so the method of teaching by similitudes and parables, which has been in use from the most remote antiquity, serves admirably as an instrument of convenient explanation and agreeable instruction, whatever the subject. But after the discovery of mirrors came the useful invention of those other instruments, the optic tubes, which examine an object not by reflection but by direct scrutiny, even more searchingly than is possible for ordinary vision. Hence we must rely on them when we require a distinct view of remote or minute objects. In like manner the very natural method of syncrisis is properly followed by the analytic and synthetic methods, which examine what an object is in itself by taking it apart and then putting it together again.

66. From the preceding it follows that analysis, synthesis, and syncrisis kindle the mind to an enlightened understanding of things and that anyone trained in these methods cannot fail to grasp things intelligently. Hence the rule:

C. *When we seek exact knowledge of things, we must combine the analytic, synthetic, and syncritic methods.*

Note that we must combine them, not confuse them. First the analysis must be completed as a whole; corresponding and antithetical parts must be outlined and defined at the same time, before we proceed to a synthetic treatment of individual parts. Herein lie many of the secrets of teaching, which will be explained in the appropriate place. (This is further touched upon in Sec. 153 below.)

67. So much for comprehension. Judgment is an inward weighing of things; hence it functions in exactly the same way as external weighing: by means of a pair of scales, and two things weighed against each other, and an observant, appraising eye.

68. The pair of scales is a particular method of judging, which considers things in relation to their exemplars; that is, it always poses two questions simultaneously: what (or of what kind, how great, where, how, etc.) a thing is and whether it should be that (or of that kind, so great, there, in that manner, etc.). Thus the two matters weighed in judgment are an ideated thing together with its idea. The eye taking note of the equilibrium (or of the excess or deficiency of weight on one side or the other) is reason, the inner eye of the mind, which compares thing with thing. Let us illustrate: if someone shows you a picture which he says is the likeness of this or that person, you cannot judge whether it is a likeness if you do not know the person whose portrait it is supposed to be. But, if you do know him, you can easily pronounce judgment by comparing the features of the portrait with those of the original (ectype with archetype). And that is precisely what happens in all situations where we pass judgment (unless we judge at random): we compare the thing exemplified with the exemplar, as, for instance, when we judge an act according to a commandment or a law.

Axioms:

CI. *To know the exemplars of things is the foundation of judgment.*

CII. *To compare things with their exemplars is the act of judgment.*

CIII. *To compare things with their exemplars rightly and then to pronounce a right opinion is the completion of judgment.*

Corollaries: Therefore,

1. Unless we first know the exemplars of things, our judgment is worthless.

2. Unless we know things and compare them with their exemplars, our judgment is mere prejudice.

3. If we examine things carelessly or compare them carelessly with their exemplars, our pronouncements are a miscarriage of judgment.

But much more of a miscarriage if we pronounce judgment without knowing the exemplar or evaluating the example.

69. Hence it follows that if you wish to enlighten the mind of a student in such a way that he will be able not only to comprehend things but also to form judgments about them, you must acquaint him with the exemplars of things (which are the perfect forms of things) and instil in him the habit of performing whatever comes his way according to its appropriate exemplar. If you do this properly, you will make him truly capable of judgment. Therefore,

CIV. *We should establish the universal forms and norms of things and show how they guide us in dealing with each particular thing.*

70. So much for the refining of judgment. Various aids for the strengthening of memory have been discovered; even pictures and artificial devices have been employed in a variety of experiments and demonstrations that have accomplished extraordinary results, as teachers of mnemonics attest. But these devices are considered a violent procedure, enfeebling the judgment, which is man's distinguishing faculty, and turning out parrots that repeat borrowed thoughts and produce nothing valuable of their own. If this is true (we do not assert it but do have our suspicions), we must look for safer aids, which will assist the natural powers of memory and not harm the judgment. (For it is a bad medicine that destroys something natural.) To find these aids, we must first of all consider what memory is and how the act of memorizing is carried on, in the hope that we may thus discover some gentle means by which to aid it.

71. Memory is the supplying faculty of the mind, which receives whatever is grasped by the senses, preserves it, and then produces it when there is need.

72. Its functions are threefold: to store up, preserve, re-

produce, that is, to grasp, retain, and give back. If it stores up carefully, preserves faithfully, and gives back readily, we call it a good memory; contrariwise, if it allows useful matters to pass it by or escape it altogether and therefore does not reproduce them or does so slowly and imperfectly, we call it a bad memory. But even in the same person all these three faculties are not to be found in equal measure. Indeed, some persons receive impressions easily but also lose them easily; others receive them with difficulty but retain them long; still others forget easily and recall easily. Because of this diversity in aptitudes, the memory has need of divers aids, which may help it sometimes to receive impressions, sometimes to retain them, sometimes to recall them.

73. Generally, however, it will be found true that no one can reproduce what he has not memorized or memorize what he has not first imprinted in his mind. Likewise is it true that, the firmer the impression, the stronger will be the retention and the easier the recollection. Hence these axioms:

CV. *What you wish to remember, first imprint in the memory.* For no one can remember or recall what he has never imprinted in his memory by deliberate thought.

CVI. *The more permanently you wish to remember anything or the more readily you wish to recall it, the more deeply you must imprint it in the memory.*
Whatever touches the senses casually and therefore makes only a slight impression on the mind is easily blotted out.

CVII. *Strength of memory derives primarily from strength of impression.*
Consequently, our primary consideration is to see how impressions are made. But the process of retaining and the process of recalling impressions also have their own special aids. Therefore, let us examine each process separately.

74. An impression is a mental representation of anything that has been grasped by the senses.

> Just as in writing these words, I conceive their images in my mind and with my hand transmit them to a pen and with the pen to paper, in order to make their likenesses take shape here, even so the images of this writing imprint themselves on your eye, Reader. And then your eye transmits them to your mind (that is, to your understanding and hence to your memory),[7] where they fix themselves in such a way that your mind can contemplate them even when their material forms are no longer present. The more purely these images have been abstracted from material things and the more firmly they have been impressed on the mind, the better. Now let us see what means can aid that impression to become stronger.

75. In general, three things aid impression: careful perception (which depends on the senses), clear understanding, and accurate discernment.

CVIII. *Aids to perception, understanding, and judgment are also aids to memory.*

> Indeed, it is impossible not to remember what one has grasped with his senses so carefully that he understands it and even can pass judgment on it. On this point Erasmus remarks, "A large part of memory consists in deep understanding."[8]

Corollary: Therefore, if one heeds the evidence of his senses, employs the instruments of his understanding accurately, and distinguishes things carefully, such a person cultivates his memory well and finally achieves a strong memory.

76. Specifically, if we consider the objects of memory, there are three aids to impression: clarity, order, and par-

---

7. The passage within parentheses was added in the Amsterdam edition.

8. Erasmus, *De ratione studii:* "Bona memoriae pars est rem penitus intellexisse."—Reber. Comenius substitutes *magna* for the *bona* of Erasmus.

ticularization. If we consider ourselves, there are seven: an unoccupied mind, tranquillity, strong sensibilities, individual observation, leisurely reflection, repetition, and, finally, discussion.

77. Clarity is necessary because, if an object stands out clearly, it will also strike the senses clearly and will be impressed upon them so clearly that it can be understood, then judged, and then committed to memory. Therefore,

CIX. *Whatever does not make sense can be neither understood nor appraised*[9] *and hence cannot be committed to memory.*

> For example, a sentence, even the most elegant, spoken to me in Turkish.

Corollary: Whatever is to be committed to memory should be clear.

78. Order in subject matter is essential if we are to perceive how well the various parts of a subject hold together, so as to impress them on our memory in the exact order in which they follow one another. Therefore,

CX. *Whatever lacks coherence is difficult to understand and to judge; for the same reason it is also difficult to commit to memory.*

> For example, suppose I utter separately these four words in a language with which I am acquainted: *soul, is, thing, order.* As they stand, they are a hodgepodge; but, when arranged in some rational order (e.g., "order is the soul of things"), the better they cohere among themselves, the better they adhere to the understanding and to the memory.

Corollary: Whatever is to be committed to memory should be orderly.

CXI. *Just as order in things is the basis of understanding and judgment, so also is it the basis of memory.*

> Because order in things and words makes for orderly conceptions in the mind, since mental concepts are nothing but

9. *Appraised* is here used as a compromise between the *diiudicari* ("distinguished, discerned") of the Leszno edition and the *iudicari* ("judged") of the Amsterdam edition.

mental images of things and words. For that reason I believe that we cannot devise a better aid to memory than to reduce things and words to their natural order. Indeed, the mind, of its own accord and even against man's will, pursues its noble impulse toward the reality of things as long as it is not retarded, repulsed, or perplexed by a confused mass of things (or words).

79. Particularization is necessary, since the cause of a thing, its effect, place, time, and similar data are like so many handles by which I can grasp that thing and hold it the more firmly.

CXII. *When particulars are lacking, it is almost impossible to understand or judge a matter and equally impossible to commit it to memory.*

Corollaries: 1. Whatever is to be committed to memory should be well defined by particulars.

The more of these, the better. And since causes are the most significant particulars, to understand causes is, as it were, to drive a thing into the memory with a nail. (See Axiom XC.) Therefore,

2. Whatever is to be firmly committed to memory should be explained through its causes.

80. An unoccupied mind is one not yet filled with images, as are the minds of children, who have as yet experienced little. Such a mind Aristotle compared to a blank tablet on which nothing has yet been written but all things can be written.[10] A clean tablet or paper receives all impressions readily, but one that has been written on admits no more than there may be room for and even then confuses what was written earlier with what has been recently added. Even so is it with our minds. I know, of course, that this comparison is not valid in all respects, since the space on a sheet of paper is limited, whereas the mind, being the reflec-

10. *De anima* iii. iv. 430a: ". . . as if a tablet not yet written on were potentially written on; this happens with the mind."

tion of the infinite God, possesses infinite capacity. Nevertheless, experience shows that, the more images there are in the mind, the more often, the more readily, and the more persistently they become mixed and confounded, until they obscure and even obliterate one another, unless order and other aids are present. Therefore, let this still remain an axiom:

CXIII. *First impressions are lasting.*

For instance, what we learn in childhood, or early in the morning after sleep when the senses are alert, or in the first contact with anything whatsoever.

81. A tranquil mind is one not distracted by a throng of objects but directed toward one thing alone, as when a man is disturbed neither externally by activities nor internally by feelings. The more objects a mind is concerned with, the less attentive is it to individual objects; it grasps neither this nor that correctly but is moved by its own impulses of anger or hatred, so that it does not heed facts, except in a confused way. But a mind fixedly intent on one thing penetrates it and receives a fixed impress therefrom.

CXIV. *Impressions received through heedful observation are very lasting.*

Hence retirement and solitude, where no noise disturbs the mind, are friends to the Muses.

82. The sensibilities become stronger when the treatment of a subject involves something that strikes the mind with admiration, delight, disgust, shame, or fear. When anything strikes the senses in this way, it lodges deep in the mind, like an inflicted wound, and is not easily dislodged.

CXV. *Impressions received by a mind affected by emotion are deep and lasting.*

Corollary: Whatever amuses and stirs the mind during the process of learning is an aid to memory.

Because it tickles the mind into excitement, and excitement rouses the mind to attention.

83. Individual observation enters in when, not content to rely on the evidence of others, we try to experience things through our own eyes, ears, noses, and hands. Here lies a powerful source of true and solid impressions. Whoever has once gazed on Rome with his own eyes will have a better and a more lasting impression of the city than a thousand descriptions could give. The same thing holds true for the other senses in every respect. (See Sec. 54.) Therefore,

CXVI. *The best impressions are gained direct from things themselves.*

84. Leisurely reflection consists in detaining the mind on the same object until the mind becomes familiar with the object in its entirety. Such familiarity with the object comes from repeated observing or hearing and from accurate observation of every detail. Above all, then, bear this in mind: if you wish to imprint anything deep in the memory, do not merely read and reread it but also copy and recopy it. It is said that Philip Melanchthon used to transcribe any author with whom he wished to make himself particularly familiar.[11] For the same reason Alphonso, king of Aragon, often copied the holy scriptures with his own hand.[12]

11. For this story Reber refers us to Camerarius, *De vita Philippi Melanchthonis narratio.* Joachim Camerarius (1500–1574), humanist, biographer, and leader in the Reformation; aided Melanchthon in drawing up the Augsburg Confession; reorganized the universities of Tübingen and Leipzig; made Latin translations of Homer, Herodotus, Sophocles, Xenophon, Demosthenes, Theocritus, and other Greek authors; chiefly known for his critical edition of Plautus (1552). Cf. J. E. Sandys, *History of Classical Scholarship,* Vol. II.

12. Bart(holomaeus) Fazius, *De rebus gestis ab Alphonso* (Leyden, 1560). —Reber. Bartolomeo Fazio studied Greek and Latin under Guarino of Verona; engaged in learned disputes with Lorenzo Valla; Fazio's posthumous

CXVII. *Leisurely reflection fixes the impression of an object.*
Thus it has been well said that we should read a thing once
to find out what it contains; a second time, to understand it;
a third time, to imprint it on our memory; the fourth time
we should repeat it silently to test ourselves whether we have
firmly mastered it. More of this in the next paragraph.

85. Repetition consists in restating to ourselves or de-
scribing and showing to someone else what we have just
seen, heard, read, or contemplated. The first method is a
good way of fixing the impression, but the second is better,
because if you teach another what you yourself have
learned, not only do you repeat the material by reviewing it
in your consciousness, but now that you are contributing
something of your own, as it were, you treat the material
more energetically and thus, so to speak, you assert your
mastery of it. Experience proves this. Hence the following
axiom:

CXVIII. *To retrace an impression is to strengthen it.*

86. Discussion consists in repeating what we have learned
and testing ourselves whether we have learned it correctly.
This we can do for ourselves or with the help of another.
Ten consecutive readings do not imprint a piece of writing
on the memory so well as do four or five readings between
which you endeavor to recite the matter from memory,
consulting the book when memory fails. Similarly, if you
describe, commend, or expound a subject to another person,
you will never be sure whether he has grasped it, though you
repeat yourself a thousand times; but you will quickly make

De rebus, translated into Italian by J. Mauro, was printed in Venice in 1580.
The reference is to Alfonso V (1385–1458), called *the Magnanimous;* king
of Aragon (1416–58); as Alfonso I, king of Sicily (1416–58) and king of
Naples (1443–58); patron of Renaissance men of letters; carried Livy or
Caesar with him on campaigns; delighted in coarse flytings of scholars,
whom he trusted to preserve his fame.

sure, if you question and examine him to test the degree of his comprehension. For he will be more attentive and vigilant if he fears that he will be questioned, and he will learn better for fear that his lack of comprehension will be detected; thus his self-esteem will make him redouble his efforts to pay attention.

CXIX. *To probe and test an impression is to reinforce it.*

87. So much for the strengthening of impressions. The power to retain impressions is chiefly aided by constant repetition, of which it has been rightly said: "Frequent review is more potent than any artificial aid," and also, "Repetition is the father and mother of memory." For it is impossible to obliterate that which is being continually renewed.

CXX. *Repetition is an antidote against forgetfulness.*
Whether the repetition consists in silent rereading or oral recitation or any other exercise whatsoever.

88. Another aid to the retentive power of memory is writing, by which we reimprison, so to speak, what the senses have captured. From this second imprisonment our memories cannot flee and escape, as they do from the brain, but can be produced whenever needed. Writing is a wholly indispensable prop without which the memory simply would not be equal to rather extensive and involved subjects. After all, what mortal would trust his memory to encompass whole speeches or books, astronomical calculations, and similar materials?

CXXI. *Writing is a storehouse of repetition.*
For whatever has been committed to writing can be repeated; that is, it can be recovered for use. One way of doing this is to mark and identify memorable passages for ourselves by annotating the margins of the books we read or by underscoring important points with colored lines, so

that we may more easily remind ourselves on which sheet of a book, on which page of the sheet, in what part of the page or line such and such a passage appears. Another way is to transcribe significant passages at the beginning or the end of the book, or to paint them on the door and on the walls, or to cut them into windowpanes, etc., so that they will be ever before our eyes. A third way is to compile our own lists and records to serve for daily review, or digests and commonplace books to serve as general registers of subjects in which we file and arrange all that is worthy of note. Since books of this sort are repositories of memory, they not only provide a wealth of material for research but also assemble the most acute judgments in one place.

89. Let us put in the third place the more artificial aids to memory: namely, the transformation of (1) the intelligible into the perceptible, (2) the uncomprehended into the comprehended, and (3) the unlimited into the limited.

90. The intelligible is rendered perceptible through symbols and parables. Thus the functions of a good judge are represented by the figure of a blindfolded maiden bearing scales in one hand and a sword in the other to show that she does not regard persons but weighs issues. Once a person understands what the various parts of this picture denote, he can hardly ever forget the duties of an upright judge. This is the reason for all parables and fables as well as for most proverbs and figures of speech; it is a basic device in the art of memorizing.

CXXII. *Symbolic representation of things is the key and the keystone of memory.*

91. To reduce the uncomprehended to the comprehended serves most usefully when you try to memorize strange names. Your memory will retain more easily and more surely the word *Alabandensis* ("of Alabanda," a city in Asia),[13] if

13. A city in Asia Minor, in the province of Caria, famous for its commerce and notorious for its morals.—Reber.

you already know and think of these three words: *ala* (Latin "wing"), *Band* (German "band"), and *ensis* (Latin "sword"); so too with *Califurnia*, a region in America, if you imagine a hot furnace (Latin *calentem furnum*). All etymologies, if they are true and not merely playful, work to this end; they bring to the study of languages facility, pleasure, and substance.

CXXIII. *Comprehension, of whatever kind, is the light of memory.*

Corollary: But true comprehension is a blazing light of memory.

92. To reduce the unlimited to the limited is useful for subjects that perplex and confuse the mind with their multitude and variety unless they are confined within limits by being reduced to number and measure. We can accomplish this by breaking up masses into units, distributing extensive materials into graduated steps, reducing the complex into the simple, relating the particular to the general, joining the remote to the near, and reducing the irregular to the regular, as we noted in Section 45 and the following.

CXXIV. *Partition of the unlimited is a great instrument of memory.*

This is indeed the origin and basis of all theories, rules, and systems, because this is the way in which the unlimited is forced within the limited confines of the mind.

93. So much, then, for the retentive powers of memory. Recollection takes place when a present experience brings back to mind a past experience with which it has something in common.

As when we encounter or hear mentioned some object, person, or place that reminds us of some similar, different, or exactly contrary sight, sound, or deed at some time or other, in some place or other.

CXXV. *Recollection depends on occasion.*

For just as man does nothing and says nothing, asks nothing and answers nothing, without occasion, so he neither thinks nor reflects without occasion.

Corollary: Therefore, we should provide occasions that will recall what is useful.

94. These occasions, which rouse the memory and evoke some of its hidden treasures, are to be found in the coherence of things, because coherence in things brings with it coherence in thoughts. For everywhere thing coheres with thing; indeed, all things are connected. This is illustrated by the way causes are related to effects and effects to causes; such too is the relation of form to matter, ends to means, attribute to substance, parallel to parallel, difference to difference, contrary to contrary. In a word, everything is related to its counterpart; thus, when one is posited, the other is also posited. In like manner words join themselves to words in discourse; if one is uttered, others must follow, as is required by the need for completeness of thought, by the laws of composition, and, finally, by the rules of meter and rhythm. In exactly the same way thoughts (which are nothing but images of things and words) link themselves to one another, so that notion tugs at notion, just as in a chain one link pulls another. For whenever a fresh notion originating in a present sensation enters the storehouse of memory, another notion, its parallel, immediately hastens to meet it and receive it. But the second notion brings in its train another parallel, and the latter in turn brings up other parallels. Indeed, just as in nature there exists no vacuum and thing impinges upon thing, so is it with thoughts.

CXXVI. *Occasions for recollection are linked as in a chain.*

Corollary: Therefore, they should be treated as links in a chain. (That is, whatever the subjects being studied, they should be combined in such a way that the recollection of one will bring with it the recollection of another, and so on.)

95. And since memory works forward, not backward (being nourished, of course, not by what is past but by what is to come), things and our notions of things should be linked not in a capricious fashion but in such a way that the known comes first and ushers in the unknown. (Which one of us, if asked what follows in the Lord's Prayer after the words "Our daily bread," would not immediately answer, "give us today"?[14] If asked, however, what precedes the words "Our daily bread," would not everyone be at a loss? Nor would anyone be able to answer except by recalling what precedes the words in question.) Hence the complaint of Stephen Ritter[15] about his experience with pupils using a Latin-German dictionary with these rhyme-tags: *Deus— Gott, necessitas—Noth; unitas—Einigkeit, trinitas—Drei- faltigkeit;* etc. When he asked the Latin word for *Gott*, one student did not know, but another answered, *"Necessitas."* There is nothing surprising, insolent, or impudent in this answer; because of the reasons which we have just re- counted, the answer was inevitable. Therefore,

CXXVII. *The occasion or starting point of recollection should be the known; the object of recollection should be the less known.*

For we do not learn the known by way of the unknown but the other way around, according to Axiom V.

14. In Latin the order of words is
      "Panem nostrum cotidianum da   nobis hodie"
      "Bread our   daily   give us   today."

15. *Vocabularium Germanico-Latinum scholarum comitatus Waldecensis* (Kassel, 1620), Preface.—Reber. This is perhaps the Ritter mentioned, along with Ratke, Lubin, Helwig, Bodin, and others, in the prefatory Greet- ing of the *Didactica magna* (par. 10), as one of the enlightened teachers of the "newly rising" age. Keatinge (II, 303) identifies him wrongly, I believe, with a Franciscus Ritter. Versified textbooks were a heritage of the Middle Ages; Eberhard of Bethune (*fl.* 1212) and Alexander of Ville-Dieu (d. 1240) composed elementary grammars in Latin verse. Alexander's *Doctrinale* was popular as late as the fifteenth century.

96. So much for the method of imparting knowledge with the dependable assistance of understanding, judgment, and memory; the method of inculcating prudence will be discussed next.

B. THE METHOD OF TEACHING PRUDENCE

97. By prudence we mean the skill to conduct one's self rightly in the midst of perplexities (that is, to choose the beneficial and to avoid the harmful). This whole problem lies in the domain of our will, which, so to speak, is the arbiter of our actions. The will, being by its very nature completely free, neither desires to be nor can be forced; it obeys only its privy councilor—reason. Therefore, we should try not to force but to persuade the will to desire the good which nature desires and to repudiate the evil which nature repudiates.

98. Hence this method is grounded on both theory and practice. Theory should indicate precisely the differences between good and evil and show how the final outcome of good is always happy; that of evil, always sad. If this is done properly, it follows that good will be chosen and evil will be shunned,[16] because it is most natural[17] for every

16. This notion, that man chooses evil only through ignorance and embraces good if he knows how to measure good, underlies the Comenian as well as the Socratic and Platonic ideal of "education." Cf. comment on Axiom XL, above, and Plato *Protagoras* 357.

17. By *nature* and *natural* Comenius does not mean the warring "natural condition" of mankind, as conceived by Hobbes, or the gentle "state of nature" portrayed by Rousseau. His view of the Fall is Calvinistic, but his view of human destiny is, like Bacon's, persistently melioristic. Comenius resolves the problem in chap. v, par. 1, of the *Didactica magna* (Keatinge's trans., II, 40): "By the word *nature* we mean, not the corruption which has laid hold of all men since the Fall . . . but our first and original condition, to which as to a starting-point, we must be recalled. It was in this sense that Ludovicus Vives said, 'What else is a Christian but a man restored to his own nature, and, as it were, brought back to the starting-point from which the devil has thrown him?' (Lib. i, *De Concordia et Discordia*.) In this sense, too, must we take the words of Seneca, 'This is wisdom, to return to nature

creature to desire his own good and to avoid his own destruction. On the other hand, no one desires an unknown good, and no one flees from an unknown evil. Ludovicus Vives[18] aptly remarks that in human life there is nothing more pernicious than that corruption of judgment which fails to give things their proper value. Because of it we pursue the

---

and to the position from which universal error (that is to say, the error of the human race, originated by the first men) has driven us,' and again, 'Man is not good but becomes so, as, mindful of his origin, he strives toward equality with God.' (Epist. 93.)"

18. The great Spanish humanist Juan Luis Vives (1492–1540); professor of humanities at Louvain and lecturer at Oxford; friend of Erasmus and Thomas More; prominent scholar at the court of Henry VIII and friend of Catherine of Aragon. Like Comenius, an admirer of Aristotle but a severe critic of Aristotelity and scholasticism in the universities; attacked abstruse theological disquisitions couched in barbarous Latin, as at the University of Paris. One of the first writers on the scientific study of pauperism; precedes Bacon and Descartes in advocating the inductive method and the study of psychology. In *De anima et vita* (1538) discusses association of ideas, the nature of memory, mnemonics; interested not in metaphysical deliberations about the essence of the mind but in the manifestations of the actions of the mind; an early pragmatist, insisting that knowledge is of value only when it is put to use. His most important work, *De disciplinis* (1531), in three parts and twenty books, includes (I) *De corruptis artibus*, seven books; (II) *De tradendis disciplinis*, five books; (III) *De artibus*, eight books. The *De causis corruptarum artium*, in the first part, is ranked with Bacon's *Novum organum* as one of the greatest contributions to the new science and philosophy of the Renaissance and is considered a landmark in modern educational reform. The second part of the *De disciplinis* deals with the teaching of language and was highly regarded by Comenius. The third part outlines methods of instruction that anticipate those of Comenius: state-supported schools in every community for students of all classes and of both sexes (though girls and boys must not be taught together); instruction according to capacity; avoidance of harsh punishment; inductive procedure; graded instruction whereby one lesson logically introduces the next; trained teachers with sufficient pay, so that they may actually be moral examples to their students and not slaves to ambition and covetousness; ambition unfits a man for teaching. For somewhat similar views on remuneration for teaching see Bacon, *Advancement of Learning*, Book ii, par. 9. For a detailed study of Vives and an extensive bibliography see Adolfo Bonilla y San Martin, *Luis Vives y la filosofía del renacimiento* (Madrid, 1903).

worthless as though it were worthy and reject the worthy as though it were worthless; that is, we act imprudently, foolishly, and dangerously.[19] Augustine also rightly says: "We love good in so far as we know it," and conversely, "We hate evil in so far as we understand it." Therefore,

CXXVIII. *To understand rightly what is beneficial and what is harmful constitutes the basis of prudence.*

> Consequently, if you would prevent a person from transgressing through imprudence, see to it that he is not ignorant of anything which concerns him. He will thus become prudent; or if he does transgress, he will transgress to his own harm.[20] (See Axiom XL and the commentary thereon.)

99. But practice is necessary, and practice demands examples and imitation (and correction),[21] according to Axioms XXXV, XXXVII, and XLVII.

CXXIX. *To choose the beneficial and to avoid the harmful constitutes the act of prudence.*

100. But since there are many things which affect us indifferently, that is, do not particularly aid or particularly hinder useful activity, it is an act of prudence neither to seek after them painstakingly nor to flee them in superstitious fear.

CXXX. *To make indifferent use of what is indifferent constitutes a supplement to prudence.*

19. Paraphrased from the beginning of the third book of *De tradendis disciplinis*, a work which constitutes the second part of the *De disciplinis*. Reber notes a similar passage in the first part of the *De disciplinis*, in the second book, i.e., *De causis corruptarum artium:* "Indeed, too much attention to stories and fables, in so far as they contain foolish and disgraceful matter, disturbs the mind, stultifies the judgment and other important faculties, and takes possession of the memory to the exclusion of more useful matters."

20. The text reads "aut si peccabit, suo malo peccabit." I take it that Comenius means "for he will know that if he transgresses, he transgresses to his own harm."

21. The words in parentheses were added in the Amsterdam edition.

C. THE METHOD OF WORKS

101. This method requires theory, prudence, and practice. Theory is necessary, so that a man, no matter what he does, will not do it like a brute, on blind impulse, but with an understanding of what he is doing. Such understanding inevitably brings with it caution and vigilance not to err in his work, and constant practice finally makes him incapable of error. Therefore,

CXXXI. *Let theory always come before practice.*
That is, elementary theory before elementary practice, advanced theory before advanced practice.

CXXXII. *Let prudence always accompany practice.*
Otherwise, if he does not watch himself and his own actions, even a man of understanding may fall into error. Therefore,

CXXXIII. *Let practice always bring practice to perfection.*
Doing cannot be learned except by doing. Hence the saying, "We create by creating." One becomes a writer by writing, a painter by painting, a singer by singing, a speaker by speaking; and so it is with all external acts. So too one learns perseverance by persevering, endurance by enduring, abstinence by abstaining, courage by striving and acting courageously, etc.; and one learns these qualities sooner and better by practicing them than by discussing them or analyzing ways of attaining them.

102. The theory of getting things done consists in knowing what, by what means, and in what way a thing is to be done. The learner will readily know what is to be done if you show him an exemplar; by what means and in what way, if you tell him what the implements are and how they are to be employed or if you demonstrate their use. It is better, however, to do both. See Axioms XXXV–XLII, which for our present purposes can be summed up in this single axiom:

CXXXIV. *When a pupil is to perform something, present him*

with an exemplar, show him the implements, and teach him how to imitate.

103. A pupil learns to act with circumspection and prudence if he imitates accurately and if the teacher constantly watches over the pupil to prevent him from error in his first attempts. If the pupil does err, the teacher should warn and correct him, giving reasons for the reproof and for the correction, according to Section 33 and Axioms XLV and XLVII.

CXXXV. *A beginner is never to be relied upon and for that reason should be watched lest he fall into error.*

> The pupil should not trust himself, nor should the teacher trust him. It is true that some pupils are so industrious that even when left to themselves they sometimes work correctly; this, however, is rare and does not outweigh the damage which results when a pupil left to himself acquires the habit of faulty workmanship. This is so because bad habits breed bad practices just as good habits breed good ones, and to discard a habit (that is, to unlearn) is a laborious task, according to Axioms LVI and LVII. (For just as good citharists develop by playing the cithara well, so bad ones develop by playing it badly.) In order to lighten his own work and that of his pupil, the teacher should set forth the first outlines of the subject accurately and take special pains to make sure that the pupil's first attempts at reproduction are as accurate as possible. Note that, if the teacher always does this in the initial stages, he will quickly make an end of difficulties for himself and for his pupil, and both will find pleasure in the later stages of the undertaking.

104. Furthermore, if a person has once done something correctly, it is impossible for him not to be able to do it a second time; in fact, the more often he does it, the more surely and easily can he do it again. Thus it comes about that every subject, of whatever kind, demands frequent

practice; in other words, a habit is not established by one or two performances. Therefore,

CXXXVI. *In every art there should be more practice than theory.* That is to say, even one demonstration is enough to make us perceive what is to be done and how it is to be done, but only frequent repetition will enable us to do it in the prescribed and indicated manner. An example is like a seed, a precept like the harrowing in of a seed, and exercises are like showers, winds, and sunny days. One throw suffices to commit the seed to the earth, and no great length of time is required to bury the seed in the bowels of the earth by drawing the harrow lengthwise, crosswise, and athwart; but months of frequently recurring showers, sunny days, and winds are required to make the seed sprout forth, grow, and ripen. In like manner, even a single good demonstration will enable you, if you are attentive, to understand a mode of operation, but only frequent practice will give you the skill to perform the operation.

Corollary: We must insist on faultless practice until there is no danger of error.

105. And since whatever develops, develops by the synthetic method (from lesser to greater, from simpler to more complex, etc., according to Axiom LXXIV and its corollary), the first attempt at imitation should never start with a finished work but with rudimentary parts, and these should be the smallest and the simplest. In this way progress will be easy and sure.

CXXXVII. *Practice should begin with the smallest, not with the largest; with parts, not with the whole; with rudiments, not with finished works.*

For example, when a person is learning to read, he does not begin with a text, or words, or syllables, because he is unable to do so; he begins with single letters. This procedure should be followed everywhere.

D. THE METHOD OF LANGUAGES

106. From the preliminary theory of language which we treated in chapters i, ii, iii, etc.,[22] it is apparent that the method of languages is more difficult than the method of knowing and working, because of three reasons. In the first place, the subject of every art and science is something peculiar to itself, restricted within its own limits, whereas language as a whole, even a single language, requires an understanding of all things, sciences, and arts.[23]

107. Second, whatever is required in sciences and arts is also required in the study of language and that in a somewhat larger measure. In other words, what is to be known need only be learned, and what is to be performed must be learned and then reproduced; language, however, must be learned and reproduced twice—with pen and mouth. First it is necessary to understand a language, an achievement of no great difficulty; then it is necessary to reproduce it in writing, a task somewhat more difficult, but not too difficult because it is done slowly and deliberately, especially when there is time to reflect and to consult books. But to speak a language is something of an extemporaneous achievement and therefore the ultimate that we can hope for, ask for, and attain in this study.

108. Finally, the individual problems peculiar to languages are more involved than those in the arts and sciences. The first obstacle to the understanding of languages is the astounding confusion of homonyms, synonyms, and paro-

22. A reference to the earlier parts of the *Linguarum methodus novissima;* see our Introduction for an outline of these chapters.

23. Although Comenius may not have been acquainted with Ronsard's poetic theories, his view of language as a repository of the total knowledge of man's activities is reminiscent of the French poet's advice on the scope of poetic language (cf. Pierre de Ronsard *Abrégé de l'art poétique français* [1565], par. 5).

nyms[24] in every language (of which we complained in chap.
v, Sec. 46).[25] Another obstacle lies in the variety of word
inflection and word combination peculiar to each language,
the problem being further complicated by hundreds of
exceptions. A third obstacle is the shifting and obscure
meaning of idiomatic expressions. Furthermore, almost
every language has its own special rules for orthography
and many more for pronunciation, because of manifold and
complex variations in sounds and the subtle distinctions that
the ear makes among them.

109. But we will postpone until a later chapter our discussion of how these difficulties in the study of language can
be overcome by skill founded upon method.

110. From Section 40 up to this point we have been discussing prudence in teaching as it is adapted to the requirements of the object of instruction; now follows a discussion
of prudence as it is adapted to the requirements of the
subject, that is, the pupil as an individual person. On this
point the general rule is this:

CXXXVIII. *The teacher should teach not as much as he himself
can teach but as much as the learner can grasp.*[26]

Because the learner grasps every subject according to his
capacity. A small dish will not hold so much liquid as does
a large vessel, nor can a boy understand so many things as
does a man, nor can a slow intelligence comprehend so quickly as does a quick one. That is why on one occasion when
Antisthenes concluded a rather wordy discourse, Plato remarked, "You forget that the manner of lecturing depends

24. Under this term Comenius seems to include doublets as well as
paronyms.

25. See n. 22 above.

26. One of the central doctrines in the scheme of educational reform pro-
pounded by Vives; cf. n. 18 above.

not upon the speaker but upon the hearer."[27] Likewise, then, the mode of teaching should depend not upon the teacher but upon the learner.

Corollary: Teaching adapted to the intelligence of a learner is the very lifeblood of instruction.

111. In considering our pupils, we must take into account differences in age (Sec. 112), intelligence (Sec. 115), and degree of progress (Sec. 119).

112. Age must be taken into account because boyhood excels in keenness of sense, imagination, memory, curiosity, and also the desire to be always apprehending something and doing something. Adolescence excels in the power to reason; not being satisfied with knowing that a thing exists, it busies itself with probing into what it is and why it is so and not otherwise. Finally, ripe age delights in ripe knowledge, in that abstract understanding of things whereby each thing appears as it is, without the aid of indirect reasoning. Hence we must comply with nature and permit students, whatever their level of maturity, to do that in which they find pleasure at the time.[28] In this way we shall

27. Erasmus *Apophthegmata* vii. 20; cf. Diogenes Laërtius *Vita Platonis* xxix (35).—Reber. This dominant note in the educational program of Comenius is such a commonplace in the works of rhetoricians that to seek for its immediate source is futile. Comenius may have had in mind the well-known dictum of Scaliger, whose authority he cites seven times in the *Methodus;* cf. Julius Caesar Scaliger, *Poetics* (1561), Book i, chap. i, par. 12 (Padelford's translation): "Let it be observed . . . that in deliberative and judicial speaking the orator depends upon his audience."

28. Even a casual reading of *Émile* reveals the close parallels between Comenius and Rousseau, although the latter never mentions Comenius by name and may have had no direct knowledge of his works. In fact, Comenius was largely neglected by the eighteenth century, despite praise by Leibniz and Herder; even A. H. Francke seems not to have known the *Didactica magna*. Comenius scrupulously acknowledges his borrowings, but his successors are not always so scrupulous, and therefore his direct influence is often difficult to trace.

not struggle against nature but rather act as midwives at her travail.

From this develop three rules for the first age.

CXXXIX. *The first age should be instructed only in matters that touch the senses.*

> That is, all matters should be presented to the senses in the historical manner, so that, by seeing, hearing, and touching, pupils will learn that this, that, or the other exists and develops in this, that, or the other fashion. But this is not the time to explain why a thing exists or develops in a particular way, because these pupils are not yet capable of reasoning; they are merely beginning to feel the stirrings of reason through this sensuous experience. Therefore, if you try to explain to a boy the reasons for things, you will be relating a story to a deaf person; if you try to force him to understand those reasons, you will blunt his intelligence and you will drive him to madness rather than wisdom.

CXL. *The first age should be well instructed in matters that touch the senses.*

> So as not to develop a vague, indistinct, unstable, and unnatural conception of things but rather to form a conception of things according to the patterns of things themselves;[29] for impressions received in this first age persist

29. Throughout the didactic writings of Comenius we find echoes of this Baconian principle. Constantly and specifically Comenius refers to the works of "the great Verulam." Bacon's proposals for a "philosophical" language, for a college that would "restore the sciences," and for a system of education founded on "reality," not on "empty scholastic ratiocination," stirred the thought of Comenius and motivated years of laborious endeavor on his part to make the Baconian proposals a reality. No dictum of Bacon's, however, had a more pervasive influence on Comenius' didactic writing than the well-known first aphorism of the *Novum organum:* "Man, being the servant and interpreter of Nature, can do and understand so much and so much only as he has observed in fact or in thought of the course of nature" (Spedding's trans.). It is to be noted, however, that Comenius does not subscribe to the last part of that aphorism, "beyond this he neither knows anything nor can do anything." Comenius adhered to Baconian principles only

(be they true or false, good or bad) and cannot be easily unlearned or modified (according to Axioms LVI and LVII). Therefore, we must see to it that pupils form only correct impressions.

CXLI. *The first age should be trained chiefly in those studies which depend on the use of memory.*

Studies of this sort consist of languages, music, arithmetic, geometry, and the whole range of descriptive natural history.

Corollary: Therefore, this whole age of boyhood should be guided rather by examples than by precepts.

If you want your pupils to know something, show it to them; if you want them to do something, do it while they look on; if you want them to say something, say it while they listen. They will imitate you, for they are little apes. If the imitation is not exactly right, then admonish them and correct them by means of repeated examples rather than prolonged explanations.

113. To pupils of maturer age, already trained in the experience of the senses, the following rule applies:

CXLII. *Pupils of maturer age should be introduced to the causes of things.*

So that they will not be content to know that a thing exists but will desire and will make it a habit to investigate why it is so and not otherwise.

114. The mature understanding of mature age is indicated in the following proposition:

CXLIII. *To penetrate to the true causes of many things is to arrive at a pure understanding of things.*

Especially if one comprehends the universal and supreme causes because of which all lesser ones are necessarily such or such.

115. Because of differences in natural ability a pupil may be quick or slow, keen or dull, diligent or negligent. (These

in the sphere of "historical," not "theological," knowledge (cf. pp. 128–29, n. 2 above).

differences arise from three kinds of teachableness; see Sec. 16.) If a pupil is quick, keen, and diligent, teaching proceeds without painstaking vigilance on the part of the teacher (according to Axiom XXIII). If a pupil is slow, dull, and negligent, the teacher's patience, vigilance, and diligence must come to his aid. (See Axiom XXIV.)

116. In the teaching of slow pupils this rule should be observed:

CXLIV. *Either the teacher should be not excessively talented or he should be schooled in patience.*

Cicero rightly says: "The more skilful and talented a person, the more irascibly and toilsomely does he teach; for he is tortured when he sees that what he himself grasped quickly is being grasped slowly."[30] Such a teacher, however, should remember that it is not for him to transform mental capacities but to inform them; he should remember that he cannot give to the pupil, and that the pupil cannot acquire, what has not been granted from above. He should also remember that the quicker wits are not always the best and that the slower ones sometimes compensate remarkably for their slowness if not with swift at least with solid progress. (See Sec. 14.)

117. Rule for the teaching of dull pupils:

CXLV. *The teacher should stoop to the level of the pupil and assist his power of comprehension in every way possible.*

It stands to reason that whatever is still inchoate in the pupil is already an accomplishment in the teacher. Hence the teacher should realize that, while he himself is already in the light, the pupil is just beginning to glimpse the dawn; and, therefore, the teacher should aid that dawn to break, if not quickly, at least in the right way. He can do this by not overburdening the slow pupil, by stimulating the dull pupil with many vivid examples, and by constantly rousing

30. Cicero *Pro Q. Roscio Comoedo* 11. 31. Reber notes that Comenius changes Cicero's "cum . . . percipi videt" to "arripi videns."

the inattentive pupil with fresh and diverting matter. (See the corollary to Axiom CXXXVIII.)

118. Rule for the teaching of negligent pupils:

CXLVI. *The negligence of a pupil must be offset by the diligence of the teacher.*

That is, by kindling a love of study in that pupil, by watching over him more vigilantly than over the others and, finally, by employing stimulating devices. We treated these under discipline (Sec. 38).

119. With respect to progress, pupils either have no acquaintance with the instruction they are about to receive or have already had a foretaste of it. If a pupil is totally ignorant of the subject, his instruction should begin with the rudiments; if he has had a foretaste of it, we must first see whether he has been instructed rightly or wrongly. If rightly, then let us begin instruction at the level at which we find this pupil whom we are to lead further. If badly, we must first unteach what he has learned badly, so that he will be able to learn better.

For you cannot lead an erring pupil back to the right path unless you first lead him off the wrong path. You would not pour good liquid into a vessel swarming with dregs without first emptying and cleaning the vessel; you would not superpose a picture on a painted tablet without erasing the first picture; nor would you erect a fine building without first clearing the site of earlier structures, etc. Hence in teaching it would be an act of prudence to raze what has been badly erected, that is, to make it perfectly clear to a pupil that what he has not learned in the right way is harmful, and then to build anew, that is, to teach him what is truer, better, and sounder.

120. Rule for the training of beginners who have no previous knowledge of an art.

CXLVII. *The training of the untrained should begin with the rudiments.*

Because we cannot start building a house except from the foundations. Thus a person eager to learn the art of reading must first be taught the letters of the alphabet, be he man or boy, nobleman or commoner.

121. Rule for the training of novices who are beginning to make progress:

CXLVIII. *The training of those who are beginning to make progress should proceed gradually.*[31]

It would be a wise policy to have the study of every science, art, and language divided into definite grades; and, where the subject matter is rather extensive, it should be arranged into several scales of such grades, through which pupils would be slowly guided from step to step. (See Axiom LXXVI.) The major division into grades or scales would be threefold: for those who are beginning, those who are continuing, and those who are completing their studies. Beginners are taught that which gives a foundation to knowledge; more advanced pupils are taught that which [builds up the structure; those who are completing][32] their studies add support, strength, and some degree of ornament to the structure. But each of these grades again has its minor grades, just as a lofty tower has a series of ladders provided for climbers and each of these ladders again has its steps.

122. For the progress of beginners and more advanced pupils there are these rules:

CXLIX. *Let beginners perform not many things but much of one thing; let those who are continuing or completing their studies perform not so much of one thing as a variety of things.*

31. This, one of the central recommendations in the Comenian program of reform, reflects the teachings of Vives (cf. n. 18 above).

32. The words in brackets translate three Latin words (*structuram continuant; perficientes*) omitted in the Leszno edition and supplied by Reber from the Amsterdam edition.

Because a beginner is easily confused by variety; there-fore, let him first accustom himself to one thing. As pupils advance and become more capable, they can be assigned more subjects. (See Axioms VII, VIII, and IX.)

CL. *Beginners should work strictly according to models; more advanced pupils should work without models in front of them; accomplished students should work independently.*

When little children begin to take their first steps, we do not leave them to their own devices but put them into baby-walkers. But when they become stronger and want to run about freely, we do not prevent them, because we originally shut them in not in order to keep them fettered but to give them an opportunity of learning how to walk.

CLI. *Let beginners work slowly, advanced pupils somewhat faster, and accomplished students very fast.*

For art, like nature, delights in going forward, not back-ward, and prefers to go forward slowly rather than quickly.

123. Rule for improving the instruction of those who have been taught wrongly:

CLII. *Let the training of a faulty worker begin with the removal of the fault.*

We can do this in no other way than by showing him clearly that what he has learned is faulty; we do this for no other purpose than to kindle in him a desire for truer and better things and to make him eager for a different kind of train-ing.

124. So much (from Sec. 110 on) for the special provi-sions that must be made for the instruction of various kinds of pupils. The various objectives which the teacher aims at, or should aim at, can also provide special laws of teaching. That is, the teacher ought to know how cautiously he must proceed if a student is to be taught a whole science, art, or language, and in what way to proceed if a student is to be taught only part of a subject. Likewise, the teacher must decide whether to teach in a popular style, whatever the

purpose, or meticulously for the sake of complete accuracy. Finally, he should know how to proceed when he has unlimited time as well as when, either through his own fault or the pupil's, the allotted period has been reduced, so that he is pressed for time and must hurry.

125. If only part of a subject is to be taught, instruction may begin wherever there is need or whenever opportunity presents itself; as, for example, when someone intends to travel among a people of an unknown tongue and wishes to acquire only a smattering of their language or to learn only what seem to be useful questions for the occasion, the necessary questions about directions, lodging, price of food, etc. Here any concern with method would be a waste of time; it makes no difference where you take up the subject or where you drop it.

CLIII. *A partial task is desultory, depends on circumstances, and requires no rules.*

126. If knowledge of a whole subject is desired, it is necessary to begin with foundations capable of supporting the whole mass. Once these foundations are established, we should erect upon them all that contributes to the whole structure, but in such an order that whatever precedes will form a step to what follows and whatever follows will add strength to what precedes.

> For the task of teaching is necessarily like the task of building, where nothing is erected without a foundation and every part of the superstructure rests on its own base; whatever is added to the structure is added not for the purpose of weighing down the substructure but for the purpose of strengthening it! This is accomplished if walls are built at right angles upon an ample, solid, and deep-set foundation, so that the foundation cannot give way and the walls cannot rest upon anything except their own foundations. This wise policy in the art of building is copied from the

behavior of nature itself. A plant grows only from its own seed, stands only on its own stem, and draws life only from its own roots, etc.

CLIV. *Perfect instruction must be erected on its own foundations; these should be so ample that the whole structure of teaching can be developed from them, and they should be so solid that all parts can stand through their own strength without the need of outside support.*

127. To know something in the popular way is to know or perform it as the crowd is wont to do, that is, because others say or do it thus. But to know and perform anything meticulously, in an expert fashion, is to do so with intimate comprehension of the subject. Therefore, if you wish to teach anything to anyone in the popular way, you will tell him as much as you wish him to know, and you will show him exactly what you wish him to imitate. If you wish to teach him in expert fashion, you must strictly observe all the three grades of knowledge established by the philosophers: (1) the historical, whereby we know that anything exists and that it exists thus or so; (2) the epistemonic (scientific), whereby we come to understand why anything is what it is; (3) the heuretic[33] (inventive), whereby we extract new conclusions and scientific truth from properly understood principles. For example, to understand the use of a sundial is the first or historical step in knowledge; to understand its structure and the principle on which it is built is the second or scientific step; but to understand the fundamental principle so thoroughly that we are able to

33. I retain Comenius' *heuretic* because the word indicates a shade of meaning slightly different from that of *heuristic*. The purist might also argue that *heuretic*, although rare in English, comes into the language earlier and is a more regular formation than *heuristic*. The knowledge discussed here is summed up in Auguste Comte's well-known phrase "savoir pour prévoir"; cf. E. Čapek, *J. A. Komenský: Analytická didaktika* (Praha, 1947), p. 97.

invent a new kind of sundial is the third step. The first step is easy, because it rests on experience alone, that is, on the senses. The second is more difficult, because it is arrived at through reasoning. The third is the most difficult, because it is gained only through exhaustive reasoning that leads to a pure, full, and detailed understanding of the subject. Hence the following axioms:

CLV. *He who learns in the popular way must take things on aith; he who learns as an expert must seek out reasons.*

CLVI. *Expert knowledge begins in sense-perception and ends in comprehension when reason is the intermediary.*

CLVII. *Therefore, human talent should be trained in such a way that these steps are not confused.*

That is, such training should generally take into account the age of the learner (because the first age, that of infancy and childhood, cannot be trained except by a historical or narrative treatment of subjects, with reasoning and finally pure understanding coming later, according to Axiom CXXXIX and the next four axioms). Such training should also specifically take into account the subject matter; in other words, the study of every subject should first concern itself with historical fact or *the what* (*tò hóti* in Greek), then with causes or *the wherefore* (*tò dióti* in Greek*,*, and, finally, with consequences or deductions (*porísmata* in Greek) even to infinity.

Corollaries: 1. A historical statement of a subject is the first step in knowledge.

2. An understanding of causes is the second step in knowledge.

3. A perception of consequences is the final step in knowledge.

Hence the point of the saying: Every good statesman (physician, theologian, philosopher) is a prophet, because it is given to every really wise man to foresee results in causes.

[128. If you have unlimited time for teaching a pupil, proceed gradually, omitting nothing that serves to make the task complete; if, however, you must hasten (for any urgent reason), apply yourself only to the most necessary parts. For example, if a pupil happens to be sickly and has no hope of living long but is oppressed with the fear of death, do not burden him with worldly learning, sciences, arts, or polite manners (since he may never have any use for such matters), but hasten to instil in him the art of commending his spirit to the Father and thereby the art of dying happy.

CLVIII. *If your allotted time is strictly limited, you should perform nothing except that for which there is utmost need.*][34]

34. The passage within brackets is not in the Leszno edition but is supplied by Reber from the Amsterdam edition. This insertion appears to be out of keeping with the almost purely intellectual subject matter of the *Analytica;* it is, however, closely allied to the discussion in chaps. xiv ("The School of Old Age") and xv ("The School of Death") of the newly discovered *Pampaedia.*

III

SPECIAL MEMORANDA ON HOW TO
TEACH RAPIDLY, AGREEABLY,
AND THOROUGHLY

128. Up to this point we have been discussing the fundamentals of didactics as we extracted them from its veins. If we always conduct our teaching according to these fundamental principles, we may hope to bring it about that whatever we teach will seem brief, will be pleasant, and will sink its roots deep. In Sections 3 and 4 we made these virtues of didactics our goal, and they are in truth the very soul of teaching; therefore, it is fitting to pause a moment to see whether we have already achieved our goal.

129. First of all it must be realized that the most fundamental law of our didactics (that all subjects must be taught by examples, precepts, and practice, according to Sec. 26 and the following) is nothing less than the royal road of rapidity, agreeableness, and thoroughness. Hence the axiom:

CLVIII. *Rapidity is greatly promoted by constant examples, agreeableness by clear precepts, and thoroughness by continual practice.*

> That is, to walk where another has walked is safe and easy, and to walk even in darkness is safe and easy if a bright torch is carried in front. Moreover, to walk again and again along the same path makes one feel secure.

130. But all the other parts of this didactics also tend to make instruction penetrate the mind more easily, more pleasantly, and more profoundly. At this point it is feasible

to review and summarize those parts, so that we may have more comprehensive laws for systematizing those devices of the didactics of languages which we are now prepared to elaborate.

A. CONCERNING RAPIDITY

[132. Since beginnings are usually enthusiastic, we must make every effort to complete rapidly whatever we teach or learn, so that the spirit may experience a sense of achievement and profit before the initial impulse cools down. Otherwise the spirit may relinquish the task out of vexation for not having attained its goal, or wearily plod onward, bored at the prospect of its dawdling approach to the goal. Indeed, the common saying, "Hot at the start, tepid later, and cold at the finish," is always confirmed by teachers and students who attempt to strike when the iron is not hot.][1]

131. Let us include all that specifically contributes to rapidity within seven axioms. The first of these will deal with the necessity of always keeping in view the objective of every study and of aiming solely at that objective.

CLIX. *Straight to the mark; avoid all bypaths.*

Corollaries: 1. Therefore, from the very beginning, look ahead toward the end.

> And show it to the student, so that, seeing the objective himself, he may conceive a hope that it can be reached and will become eager to reach it. For to foresee the end from the very beginning and to proceed toward it without hindrance is a delight to our spirit, which shrinks from endlessness and delays.

2. Consider the end rather than the means.

> Because means exist for an end, not for themselves; besides, they usually tend to become confused with other means, which do not make for the same end and from which we

---

1. The passage within brackets is not in the Leszno edition; it is supplied by Reber from the Amsterdam edition.

cannot easily distinguish the pertinent means except by keeping the end in view. Hence the remark of Seneca: "Consider the end and you will banish superfluities."[2]

3. Whatever leads straight to the goal should be the royal road; whatever has the appearance of a digression should be considered a delay.

To be negligent of certain things is to be commendably diligent, if those things contribute little or nothing to the purpose. When one is in haste, concern with anything but the road is a hindrance. Therefore, in theoretical subjects, do not delay over preliminary exposition but display the subject and bid the pupil examine it; then explain it and find out whether he understands it. Matters will then proceed swiftly. In teaching skills do not talk about doing something but do it[3] and bid the pupil imitate you. Warn him against mistakes; if he makes mistakes, correct him. Progress will then be completely unhindered.

132. In the choice of means, the following statement is as true and useful as it is well known:

CLX. *When few means suffice to accomplish anything, no need to use more.*

Therefore, only indispensable means should be employed; that is to say,

1. To give one example and one or two explanations of anything is sufficient; the rest may be left to practice. (See the comments on Axiom CXXXVI.)

2. "Finem specta et supervacanea dimittes." Although the *Epistulae ad Lucilium* frequently warn against superfluous learning, this particular sentence is not found in Seneca. Comenius' strictly classical *supervacanea* may be an echo of the much-repeated *supervacua* in Seneca's famous diatribe against the uselessness of "liberal" studies; cf. *Letter* lxxxviii, 36, 37, 42, 45, and particularly 35: "superfluous things (*supervacua*) must be removed from the mind." Reber believes that what appears in our text as a quotation is merely a restatement of the theme of *Letter* lxxxviii; he also notes that Seneca's admonition had prompted Vives to declaim against excessive preoccupation with miscellaneous and superfluous learning.

3. Cf. Aristotle *Nicomachean Ethics* x. 9. 1: "In practical matters the goal is not speculative knowledge of what to do, but rather the doing of it."

2. To stress fundamentals and not to dwell on petty details is the way of most rapid progress.

For example, armies intent on a swift conquest of a kingdom allow no casual obstacle to delay them but press on to the main objective.

133. Note the following rule concerning the means necessary to the attainment of a goal:

CLXI. *All means should be ready and at hand.*

If in the midst of a campaign or a battle a general were to seek for troops, arms, and other necessary equipment, he would be hastening his own downfall rather than victory.[4] But if all these are ready beforehand, he is ready for all emergencies.

Therefore, all exemplars (of what is to be known and performed), and all rules, and, finally, all instruments needed in practice should be ready beforehand.

134. But in using these materials, we must observe the following rule:

CLXII. *Always gradually, never by leaps and bounds.*

There are those who skip certain steps in order to reach their goal sooner; but, if the steps have been rightly set up, these students will surely fail of their hope, because in this way they are skipping something necessary to the understanding of what follows; and, by not rightly understanding what follows, they are setting up a barrier to the understanding of what comes even later. Thus they are forced either to remain ignorant of what they tried to learn in too much haste or to return to the beginning and this time proceed slowly and more attentively. Hence the great truth of this paradox: "Many would have reached their goal sooner, had their progress been slower." True method bids us to proceed always in such order that whatever precedes will be a step to what follows and that whatever follows will add

4. Cf. Publilius Syrus, Maxim 709: "We should provide in peace what we need in war."

strength to what precedes (see Axiom LXXVI). Therefore, if you omit any step in material so arranged, you will experience a twofold disadvantage: first, you will not supply reinforcement for what precedes; second, you will not provide a basis for what follows. Thus you will be building for ruin.

Corollaries: 1. Do not begin to teach anything unless the preceding steps have been understood.

2. Do only one thing at a time.[5]

That is, do not handle various subjects or various levels of the same subject simultaneously and you will avoid distraction, confusion, and delay. The adage rightly warns us: "He who hunts two hares catches neither." Therefore, to grasp anything, concentrate on it alone. The eye cannot be fixed simultaneously on two objects, nor can the foot rest simultaneously on two steps, but it can rest on many if it does so one at a time. (See Sec. 60 above.)

135. Nevertheless, it makes for rapid progress to take up two matters simultaneously if they are so connected that they not only can but must be taken together; that is, matters which by their very nature are so conjoined that one cannot exist, cannot develop, and cannot become known without the other. The rule for these:

CLXIII. *Always treat related matters together.*

That is, matters such as the following should be taught, learned, and practiced together: reading and writing, things and the names of things (so that I may learn to name that which I am learning to recognize, and vice versa),[6] and

5. Literally, "Whatever you are doing, do only that." Ratke and Comenius make this precept a central doctrine of methodology; both must have known the seventh maxim in the old textbook made from the sayings of Publilius Syrus: "To do two things at once is to do neither."

6. The guiding principle of the first illustrated reading book in Europe, Comenius' *Orbis sensualis pictus*, written at Sáros Pátak, 1653–54, published in Nuremberg in 1658, in London in 1659. For a critical edition of this work see *VSJAK*, Vol. X (1929). C. W. Bardeen's edition (Syracuse, N.Y., 1887)

also the theoretical and the practical knowledge of a thing (so that when you learn how to understand anything, you will also learn how to use it, and the other way around). For art without use is sterile, and use without art is aimless.

Corollary: [1. Since contraries and all opposites are also related, we should always teach them either simultaneously or close together in order to bring out the distinct nature of each.

2.][7] Since a pupil and his fellow-pupil are related beings, you will find it a short cut to rapid progress never to instruct one pupil alone but to instruct many at the same time.

It is as profitable for the teacher to kill two birds with one stone[8] as it is for the students to provide one another with examples of diligence and thus spur one another into emulation, according to the saying,

"Then does the spirited steed run well, given freedom,
When he has rivals to pass and leaders to follow."[9]

136. Although haste is the special medium of rapidity, haste consists not in headlong action but in continuous progress, even though the progress be leisurely. Therefore heed the following:

CLXIV. *Unbroken progression makes for notable progress.*

When two men are making the same journey, if one presses ahead and the other stops on the way, it is easy to see how far behind the first will leave the other in a short time. Hence, in order to reach your goal quickly, you need not force yourself, but you must apply yourself constantly; that is, as long as you are learning, let there be

1. No day without its stint.
2. No hour without a new task.

reproduces the pictures of the first edition and reprints the text of the 1727 English edition.

7. The passage within brackets is supplied from the Amsterdam edition.

8. Literally, "to whitewash two walls from the same pot," the Latin equivalent of the English saying used above.

9. Ovid *Ars amatoria* iii. 595–96; Reber notes that these verses are also quoted in the *Didactica magna*, chap. viii, par. 7.

3. No abandonment of any undertaking unless it is completed.

Because if you stop and then later come back to the work, you will not lessen your task but increase it; for you will have forgotten some part of it and will have to retrieve that loss at the cost of renewed effort. See for yourself how difficult it is to fill a cask if you let the water trickle a drop at a time, and how easy if you pour without stopping.

4. Therefore, you should not undertake at one time more than can be mastered at one stroke.

So that you will never have need to return to the same task except for the sake of repetition. But note that repetition should be used as part of a later, different operation and should serve a new purpose, as when you begin to develop later material on the basis of what has already been established.

5. No need to keep on doing what has once been done (in other words, no need to linger over what is known).

Of course, repetition is not to be neglected, partly because it gives us the pleasure of reviewing our triumphs over difficulties, partly because it reinforces the knowledge we already possess.

137. Finally,

CLXV. *Uniformity in method makes for rapidity in learning.*

And also for pleasure and thoroughness. Because when the form of the material to be treated presents no new variations, we direct our attention wholly to the substance of the material as it unfolds. In this way, when we apply the mind wholly to the material itself, we master the subject more easily and more rapidly. Besides, as long as the procedure is so clear cut, it is pleasant; and, as long as all the material imprints itself on the mind and memory so easily because of this uniform procedure (for we easily remember whatever proceeds in a familiar and a regular way), the subject will stick in the mind more firmly.

B. CONCERNING AGREEABLENESS

138. Certain observations about agreeableness of instruction should also be restated. For it is not only the poets who wish to give profit and delight but everyone who teaches effectively, because one cannot give profit without at the same time giving pleasure. Indeed, our feelings are half our being; they draw us toward objects or away from them. Where the spirit feels no attraction, it lacks inclination; and, where it lacks inclination, there it must be pushed against its will. Moreover, when the spirit is unwilling, nothing is so easy that it does not become difficult, nothing so sweet that it does not grow bitter, and nothing so good that it does not appall.

CLXVI. *We must do our utmost to guard against aversion, the most insidious poison in studies.*

139. The teacher should know how to guard against aversion, how to excite interest, and how to foster enthusiasm; he must learn this from the character of human nature itself, which spontaneously reveals what pleases it and what offends it. All this, I believe, can be reduced to seven principles. Meanwhile, let the following stand as a general rule:

CLXVII. *To deal with aptitudes as their nature demands is the basis of agreeable progress.*

To deal with them otherwise is to struggle against nature, that is, to impede, disrupt, and suppress nature's efforts.

140. In the first place, human nature is free, loves spontaneity, and abhors compulsion. Consequently, it wishes to be guided on its course; it does not wish to be pulled, pushed, or driven. That is why teachers who are morose, domineering, and given to flogging are the enemies of human nature, born with the gift to discourage and ruin native abilities rather than to encourage and develop them.[10] Here also be-

10. This passage closely parallels Montaigne's remarks on the subject in *Essais*, Book i, chap. xxv, "De l'institution des enfants." The notion that an

longs the dry and sterile dogmatist who teaches only from barren precepts and does not even divert his students enough to stimulate them but fills them with aversion and repugnance or makes them like himself, stiff and unbending. Therefore,

CLXVIII. *The teacher should never be morose in the discharge of his duties but should perform all of them with paternal kindness.*[11]

So that the pupil will feel that he is loved and will have no cause for diffidence, so that love may bind love to itself, and so that affection for persons and things may be a spur to diligence. The whole plan of our discipline is directed toward that goal. (See Sec. 37, etc.)

141. Second, human nature dreads the infinite and rejoices to perceive the limits of things. Hence it is that everything long, confused, or obscure either frightens and repels us or afflicts us with boredom. On the other hand, whatever is brief, well ordered, and clear pleases us. That is why the spirit of a man traveling to some far-off place is filled with delight when the desired end of the journey comes into view. Therefore,

---

appeal to the interests of the student helps to develop native abilities and that compulsion is harmful constitutes one of the leading principles in the method of Ratke, Comenius' senior by twenty years. But on this point Comenius was first influenced by his teacher at Herborn, John Henry Alsted, and later by his favorite author, John Valentine Andreae, to whom, in the Preface to the *Prodromus*, he acknowledges his heaviest indebtedness. The Preface to the *Didactica magna* contains a letter to which Andreae's name is affixed, perhaps wrongly; in this letter schools are described as "places of amusement, houses of delights" (cf. Keatinge, II, 19).

11. For Rousseau see Sec. 112 and n. 28 above (p. 160). Although it is difficult to ascertain how direct the influence of Comenius on Pestalozzi may have been, the passage above inevitably brings to mind Pestalozzi's dictum, "The first qualification for the task is thinking love" (cf. *Letters on Early Education* [Syracuse, 1898], p. 180). Ratke also urges the need of affection, but he is chiefly concerned with the affection that a teacher should inspire in his pupils.

CLXIX. *Let the course of every study be as brief and as well organized as possible.*

So that students will not turn hither and thither as in chaos, not knowing what is happening, whither they are going, and where they are (under such conditions the spirit is filled with dread, not with delight). But at the very beginning let them perceive the end and all that lies between, so that they will take heart and have the courage to reach that end. For surely when the human spirit realizes that everything is arranged in regular steps, so that no abysses and precipices are visible or discoverable and none need be feared along the way, it cannot but desire to push further and further ahead. Therefore, all instruction should be so devised that it offers no task for which there is insufficient time and that the prospect of what it does offer will tempt the mind of the student to plunge willingly into the work. For the mind will gladly do so when it sees some desirable addition to what it has already learned, something that can be attached as a new link to the chain that has been started; it will even desire to have something to add until the chain is completed. (See Sec. 23 above.) Accordingly, instruction will be pleasant if all assignments are reduced to easily comprehensible units, are clearly explained by word of mouth, and are immediately performed in the presence of the teacher and with the teacher's help. Nothing should be left to the demoralizing effect of solitude, for a pupil fears to be deserted and left to his own resources. But, if he sees how all present difficulties are mastered, will he not be eager to try his hand at all those that lie ahead?

142. Third, human senses delight in being linked to their objects and grieve to be separated from them, because in those objects the senses find their nourishment. That is why children (like anyone else), when they hear of something that they have never seen, heard, or tasted, eagerly rush forward to see, hear, and taste it. If you restrain them, you

crush them. Hence a method that presents everything to the pupils' senses will be a source of pleasure. Therefore,

CLXX. *We must attract our pupils by constantly appealing to their senses.*[12]

143. Fourth, human nature delights in working with things (as we indicated in Sec. 24), because, being the ordained mistress of things, it believes that to be always forming, transforming, or building something is to exercise mastery over things. Hence the difficulty of restraining it from movement and action or fettering it in any way. This natural tendency manifests itself in earliest childhood; the livelier the temperament of the child, the more vigorous this tendency. That is why it is difficult for children merely to watch what someone else is doing; they also want to do it themselves. They find no pleasure in merely listening while someone else talks; they like to interrupt and make themselves heard. Even adults count the hours as days when they listen to another's discourse (so repugnant is it to subject free thought to another's guidance). But those who are doing the talking feel no boredom, because they are freely pursuing their own thoughts. That is why our didactics allows the student full scope for practice, and rightly so. Let this be a lastng rule:

CLXXI. *Let everything be learned through individual practice.* So that work will foster skill.

144. Fifth, human nature is ever in quest of uses for things; it welcomes anything that promises to serve a useful purpose. Although it may find useless things exciting for

12. This commonplace of modern education (cf. Rousseau, Basedow, Herbart, *et al.*) is another guiding principle that Comenius shares with Ratke, although he most probably derived it from Thomas Campanella, whose anti-Scholastic writings strongly influenced him when he was a student at Herborn and at Heidelberg.

other reasons, in the long run it finds them despicable and abandons them. Therefore,

CLXXII. *Let everything be learned for use.*

We must not indulge in empty speculations;[13] let use be in evidence everywhere. Beautiful things are to be enjoyed only as they are useful, because beauty without use is a tree without fruit, show without substance, a siren that lulls the unwary.[14]

145. Sixth, human nature delights in variety and dislikes monotony. Since it was created capable of grasping infinity, it can be satisfied with no single finite thing. Therefore, as soon as it perceives or attains and accomplishes one thing, it immediately turns its desire toward something else. Hence it is that the beholder receives no pleasure from things in which all parts are alike, such things as sandy plains, the

13. Cf. Bacon's remarks on "vermiculate questions" and "fruitless speculation or controversy," *Advancement of Learning*, Book i (Spedding's ed. of Bacon's *Works*, III, 285–86), as well as the remarks on "inanes et innumeras controversias," *Novum organum*, Book i, sec. xliii; see also secs. x, xiii, liv, lix, lxiii, and lxxiii. These attacks on the "distemper of contentious learning," together with Bacon's gospel of utility and "operative" science, exercised a strong and persistent influence on Comenius, who considered the *Instauratio magna* the most illuminating philosophical work of the century, "the brightest morning-star of the age" (Preface to *Physicae . . . synopsis* [Leipzig, 1633]). See also above, n. 29 (p. 161).

14. Cf. Bacon's comments on the "distemper of delicate learning" (Spedding, III, 282–85). Comenius, of course, read the *De augmentis*, the Latin version of the *Advancement*, but for our purposes the differences between the two texts are of no consequence; hence the references here to the *Advancement*, which is readily accessible to readers of English. It may be argued that in this paragraph Comenius is merely condemning empty speculation and vain ornament; he certainly was not a strict utilitarian or an antihumanist. But the contradictions in his opinions and attitudes cannot be resolved by a simple formula or a neat arrangement of labels. The conflict in his thinking is the conflict of the Renaissance. Like many of his contemporaries, he condemns the "nude" speculations of scholasticism and the vanities of pagan art, but almost in the same breath he speculates about entities and "potestative" faculties or extols the art and also the ideas of Plautus, Cicero, Ovid, and Horace.

flat surface of the sea, a wall of unrelieved white, an empty sheet of paper, and the like. But a plain covered with trees and plants, an imposing region of mountains and valleys, fields and vineyards, towns and citadels, or a wall decorated with rich portrayals, or a paper covered with writing— what a welcome feast these are for the senses and the spirit! Therefore,

CLXXIII. *Whatever is taught should be tempered by pleasing variety.*

146. Finally, human nature (especially during youthful years) takes particular delight in games and recreations, as is shown by the way we are devoted to games during our youth and find pleasure in jests and similar relaxations of the mind throughout our lives. The reasons are not far to seek; it is natural to rejoice in freedom (see Sec. 140). Every game is something more or less voluntary and therefore an exercise of freedom, whereas occupation with serious matters has the appearance of necessity and therefore of compulsion. Furthermore, all games are social and competitive affairs, and human nature takes pleasure in rivalry, because it rejoices in praise. Finally, the human mind, eager for novelty, delights in watching the outcome of an affair (whether one's own or another's, whether serious or playful); therefore, it also loves to take part in games in which it has the opportunity of watching the outcome of a contest. That is why heavenly wisdom itself says that it plays with us (Prov. 8:30). But false wisdom is represented by the apostle James as quarrelsome and bitterly envious (James 3:14 ff.) Thus the observance of the following rule will do much to delight and to stimulate as well as to maintain enthusiasm for a task.

CLXXIV. *Whatever is studied should be studied by several pupils at the same time and under some pleasant form of rivalry.*

In our didactics we have not investigated the methods by which this can be accomplished, because they are easy to devise; perhaps we shall specify something of this sort in the proper place, that is, in chapters xiii and xxv.[15]

[Corollary: The activities of an elementary school should be a play of native talent. If we leave anything to labored and tedious learning, it will be a mockery of our new method.][16]

147. These, then, are the paths of agreeableness; if any difficulties still remain, they will melt away before the certain hope of success, which is the topic of the next section.

C. CONCERNING THOROUGHNESS OF INSTRUCTION

148. In general, the teacher should be reminded that, if he would instil sound instruction in his students, the subject he teaches must be sound, that is, of solid truth and solid worth. A solid structure will never be built from chaff, straw, hay, or sand but from stone, wood, or metal; in other words, from durable materials. Likewise, sound teaching will never be constructed from unsound notions, nor will any art transform useless knowledge into something useful. Therefore,

CLXXV. *Where solid instruction is required, we must reject trivial subjects and matters whose truth or usefulness cannot be demonstrated.*

149. But, after all, the present question concerns soundness of method, not of subject matter; therefore, let us consider how a sound method, to repeat certain earlier observations, must be based upon ten fundamentals. The first of these is that the student be eager for instruction. The parched and gaping earth readily drinks in the rain; the hungry stomach readily seizes upon, digests, and consumes food. So too an admiring love for the subject of instruction

15. A reference to later chapters of the *Linguarum methodus novissima*.

16. The passage within brackets is omitted in the Amsterdam edition.

seizes upon it with vigor and easily adapts mind, tongue, and hand to the subject in which it delights. Therefore,

CLXXVI. *Everything with gusto.*

In Sections 22 and 23 we advised how to stimulate eagerness.

150. Furthermore, when action must proceed unfailingly, the instruments of action must be unfailingly reliable, for it is hardly possible to work well with poor instruments. Now, since the instruments of instruction are examples, precepts, and exercises, it follows that the rule for sound procedure is this:

CLXXVII. *Examples should be selected for the distinctness with which they expose the subject to view, so that no part of it remains obscure. Precepts, on the other hand, should be few, clear, and universally true so that they may be safely trusted. Lastly, exercises should be patterned on an exemplar until they express it to the life.*

For, where fault serves as an example, it is quite possible to learn more faults. Likewise, where precepts or rules are numerous, wordy, involved, and subject to exceptions, it is quite probable that the mind will be daunted, disconcerted, confused, and baffled. Finally, vague imitation, attached to no exemplar, produces vague results, conforming to no idea. Therefore,

Corollaries: 1. Nothing without accurate models.

2. Nothing without infallible rules.

3. Nothing without painstaking diligence [accuracy].[17]

So that whatever is to be learned and performed will be learned and performed only in the correct way. In other words, a faulty model will produce a faulty product, an uncertain rule will give uncertain guidance, and careless imitation will render even good models and rules of little use or entirely useless.

151. The third fundamental of sound procedure is that the first foundations of teaching be solidly established. For

17. The Amsterdam edition substitutes *accuracy* for *diligence*.

all structures without foundations or with badly set foundations are built for ruin. Therefore,

CLXXVIII. *At the beginning everything should be of the very best: models, rules, attention, and, finally, the teacher himself.*

Because usually, as goes the beginning, so goes all the rest.

CLXXIX. *All beginnings should be slow but accurate: attention, perception, and, finally, imitation.* (Axioms CL and CLI.)

Precipitate haste, especially during the first stages, is usually as wasteful as negligence. Physicians know that a mistake in the first dose is not corrected by a second dose of the same medicine; mathematicians know that an error introduced into the beginning of a computation multiplies to infinity and cannot be eliminated unless we break off and return to the beginning. The Italians have aptly borrowed a proverb from architecture: "A bad foundation topples the highest towers." Therefore, unless you exercise caution at the beginning, your teaching always leaves the way open for error or creates the burden of unteaching and causes inevitable delays.

Corollaries: 1. Therefore, we should see to it that whatever is taught is rightly understood from the very beginning.

Because whatever impression the mind receives from the senses it immediately intrusts to the memory and imprints there; this impression then becomes an image difficult to erase.

2. Whatever is understood should be immediately tested to see whether it is rightly understood.

Lest the mind conceive a false image instead of reality.

3. And whatever appears to have been wrongly understood should be immediately erased, lest it take root (according to Axioms LIX and CLII).

Note well: The teacher will pluck out error effectively if, as soon as he perceives or surmises the occasion whereby the pupil fell into error, he uncovers and eliminates that occasion. For man, being a rational creature, does not even err without reason but because he is deceived by some resemblance of truth. We must therefore tear away this mask of truth, so that the erring pupil may come to know error and quickly abandon it.

152. Fourth, each succeeding layer must be carefully erected on solidly laid foundations, lest something added out of place or out of turn should totter and make all the rest totter. (Axiom XLVIII and the following.) Therefore,

CLXXX. *Unless the first layers have been firmly established, nothing new should be erected upon them.*

Otherwise you build for ruin, as some buildings show. Here applies the saying, "Not many, but much." (Axiom CLXIX.) That is, in cultivating native abilities, you should do what Pliny advises in cultivating fields: "It is more profitable to sow less and to plow better."[18] In that way you can hope for a more productive harvest with a smaller loss of seed, because those who sow much and plow little, waste much and reap little.

153. Fifth, we neither understand a subject nor make any progress in it unless we examine and work out all its essentials. Clockmaking provides a clear example: no one has a satisfactory understanding of the craft unless he understands every part needed to produce a well-regulated movement. Nor will anyone be able to make a watch unless each and every part is at hand, rightly constructed, and set in place for motion. But every whole consists of opposite ends and intervening parts, outside of which nothing exists and within which all exists; these extremes and intermediate points, when thus taken together, link themselves to one another, exert the right effect upon the senses, and educate the mind. Therefore, in teaching it is necessary to take up all these parts simultaneously and to assign them their right places simultaneously; that is, to establish the

18. Reber cites Pliny the Elder *Natural History* xviii. 19–24 (49–55), but the text of Pliny yields no exact parallel to the quotation given above.

ends first and then to fill in the intervening parts, in order to give a comprehensive view of all parts as they are linked step by step from one end to the other. When one sees and does things in this way, then indeed he sees and does them thoroughly. Therefore,

CLXXXI. *Everything fully from end to end and through all intermediate parts.*

So that at every point the student may see what is pertinent to the subject and what is not pertinent.

Corollary: Therefore, in subdividing a subject, we should take up, describe, and define all parts at the same time, so that general differences may become immediately apparent to the mind. (See the comments on Axiom C above.)

This procedure will make for great clarity. When only the first subdivision is defined and immediately subjected to extensive treatment, while the other subdivisions are postponed for later (as happens in ordinary methods), the intelligence is faced with many obscurities, delays, and knotty problems. But when opposites are plainly set side by side, they become plainly clear.

154. Sixth, to know a thing is to know it through its causes; therefore, wherever these are not self-evident, they should be explained, lest the student remain ignorant of them. That is, let a student always see not only what a thing is and how it exists but also why it could not exist in any other way. Therefore,

CLXXXII. *Everything to the core, through causes laid bare.*

That is, all parts of our subject matter should be bound together in such a way that effects flow out of causes and become intelligible in themselves. If this is done, our spirit (which Sacred Scripture calls the lamp of God) will be its own teacher, and, by uncovering the origins of things, it will of itself and for itself variously purify and magnify the light of wisdom. (See Axiom XC with its corollary and Axiom CLV and the following with their corollaries.)

155. Seventh, our senses are channels through which awareness of things flows into our minds (according to Axiom LXXXIII); hence it is inevitable that, the more senses we employ and the more often and the more accurately we employ them, the more deep-rooted does instruction become. Therefore,

CLXXXIII. *Everything through one's own senses, constantly and variously.*

So as to stir the imagination and impress it as deeply as possible (according to Axioms LXXXIV and LXXXV). That is why all the best teachers like to amplify their precepts with striking gestures, illustrations, symbols, and rituals; our master in this practice is often God himself. Thus Christ, thinking that he had not sufficiently admonished the apostles with words, placed a child in their midst and bade them imitate childlike humility,[19] which knows not how to set a value on itself. Even at the Last Supper he was not content to teach this lesson by means of words; he arose, laid aside his garment, and ministered to the apostles by washing their feet and by wiping them with a linen cloth,[20] so that the apostles could not fail to understand and take to heart what he meant. And Agabus, not deeming it sufficient to prophesy the binding of Paul, decided to bind himself with Paul's belt, in order to imprint his prophecy more deeply on the minds of his hearers.[21] (See Sec. 90.)

Corollaries: 1. Since we can end controversies and make sure of our knowledge through personal observation alone, we should submit all instruction to the evidence of the senses.

Only thus do we develop true, full, and indisputable knowledge of things. Certainly he who has once looked upon Rome, Paris, or India bears these places more firmly fixed in his mind than he who has heard them described a thousand times by others who have beheld them. A mathe-

19. Matt. 18:2–4.
20. John 13:4, 5.
21. Acts 21:10, 11.

matician, because of his own researches, knows the measurements of the heavens with greater certainty than he who merely trusts the computations of others. For the latter trusts in authority, and, if you produce an opposite authority, he immediately wavers. Hence the saying of Ecclesiasticus: "A man who has experienced much ponders much, and he who has learned much will speak of what he understands. But he who has no (direct)[22] experience has little knowledge" (Ecclus. 34:9, 10). Therefore, the whole course of study should be arranged in such a way as to give students the experience of using their own senses and reasoning powers.

2. Nor is it enough to employ one sense only once; the attention of the student should be assisted by every possible means.

3. Wherever things themselves are not available for direct presentation to the senses, they should be presented vicariously, that is, by means of pictures.

Solely for the purpose of aiding the imagination and preventing error in every possible way.

156. Eighth, many a secret of rapid and solid progress is to be found only by actual practice (for only practice develops skilled workmen); therefore, the student who has been instructed by models and rules will certainly find a key to all industry in being not merely permitted but even required to perform the work himself. This procedure also stimulates rapid progress because it makes a student see that he can advance under his own guidance (as we indicated in Sec. 143); it also keeps the senses vigorous and attentive (because it gives full sway to native ability); finally, it engenders the pleasure of repetition and thereby always leaves the mind fruitfully enriched, never barren. Hence, in urging young men to read authors for themselves and to do their own work, many an ancient was wont to say

22. *Direct* is here used to translate *coram*, which Comenius inserts into the biblical text.

that poultry has the tenderest meat not when it is fattened on prepared food but when it searches for its feed by pecking for it (*dià tò skaleúein* in Greek). Therefore,

CLXXXIV. *Everything through the constant practice of the students themselves.*

157. Ninth, the more anything is handled, the more familiar it becomes; consequently, if we would have our students well acquainted with anything and ready to use it, we must familiarize them with it through reviews, examinations, and frequent use. Therefore,

CLXXXV. *Let there be constant reviews and examinations.*

That is, our method should provide for constant practical review and testing, even during the process of learning. (What special forms this takes in the teaching of languages we shall see presently.)[23] In our tests we should look for the following:

1. Has the student learned something? This will be apparent if he can repeat it.
2. Does he understand it? This will be discovered by a variety of analytical questions.
3. Does he know how to use it? This will be revealed by prescribed but unrehearsed practice.

158. Tenth, by going back and forth, a traveler becomes well acquainted with a road; he becomes even better acquainted with it if he digresses and tries other paths and compares the various routes (in order to find out whether they are shorter or longer, more level or more arduous). Hence it will be profitable for the student not merely to go forward but also to retrace his steps and to digress; in other words, we should lead him forward, backward, and athwart. We can do this by urging him not merely to pay constant heed to the demonstrations and explanations of the teacher but also to reverse the role and to demonstrate and explain

23. A reference to chap. xi of the *Methodus*.

the same subject to others; furthermore, he ought to see and hear others besides his teacher give these demonstrations and explanations. I must make my meaning clearer by quoting a set of verses well known in schools:

Often to ask, to retain what is answered, and teach what remembered,

These are three means that will make the disciple surpass his own master.

The third part of this advice, that about teaching what we have retained, is not sufficiently well known, nor is it commonly put into practice; yet it would be highly profitable if every student were required to teach others what he himself has just learned. Indeed, there is a great deal of truth in the saying, "He who teaches others educates himself," or, as Seneca puts it, "Men learn while they teach."[24] This is so not merely because teaching strengthens their conceptions through repetition but also because it offers them opportunities of delving further into the subject. (See Sec. 85.) This is why that most highly gifted man, Joachim Fortius,[25] testifies that whatever he had merely heard or

24. "Homines, dum docent, discunt"; this quotation has no close parallel in Seneca. Reber's citation from the sixth epistle (Sec. 4) is hardly to the point: "In hoc aliquid gaudeo discere, ut doceam" ("I am glad to learn in order that I may teach").

25. Joachim Sterck (Fortius) van Ringelbergh (d. 1536?), born at Antwerp, studied at Louvain, traveled in Germany, the Low Countries, and France; painter, engraver, and author of several didactic works; Flemish humanist distinguished for originality of ideas and purity and elegance of style, professor of Greek, friend of Erasmus; planned the composition of a thousand books to be called *Chīliás*. His works, collected under the general title *Lucubrationes vel potius absolutissima kuklopaideîa*, were first printed in Antwerp, 1529; five editions. Comenius' "quotations" from Fortius, here and elsewhere in the *Methodus*, are really paraphrases and summaries of various passages in the latter's *De ratione studii;* cf. Reber, pp. 214, 364–65, 436–38, 546. Cf. also *Didactica magna*, chap. xviii, par. 44. In 1652 at Sáros Pátak, Comenius published Fortius' *De ratione studii* and also his own *Fortius redivivus*, a booklet on "how to drive laziness out of schools."

read vanished from his mind within a month. But what he had taught to others he knew as well as the fingers on his hand, and he believed that it could not be snatched from him except by death. He also suggests that a student who wishes to make great strides in learning should seek out pupils and teach them daily what he himself is learning, even if he has to hire them. It is better, says Fortius, to deprive yourself of conveniences, as long as you have someone who will listen while you teach, that is, while you make yourself proficient. That is the way he puts it. But we wish to reduce this matter to a practical rule; therefore, let us phrase it thus:

CLXXXVI. *Every pupil should acquire the habit of also acting as a teacher.*

This will happen if, after the teacher has fully demonstrated and expounded something, the pupil himself is immediately required to give a satisfactory demonstration and exposition of the same thing in the same manner. (If there are several pupils, they should do so one after another, beginning with the more talented.) Furthermore, pupils should be instructed to relate what they learn in school to their parents or servants at home or to anyone else capable of understanding such matters.

159. This practice will serve various useful purposes:

In the first place, pupils will be more attentive to every part of the teacher's exposition if they know that presently they will have to repeat the same matter and if each one fears that perhaps he will be the first to be asked to do so. (See Sec. 86 above.)

Second, by restating exactly what has been taught, everyone will imprint it more deeply in his understanding and memory.

Third, if it appears that something was not understood

quite correctly, this practice will offer an immediate opportunity for correction (on the great value of this see Axiom XLVII).

Fourth, it will enable teachers and pupils to make certain that they have grasped what they were supposed to grasp, for the mark of knowledge is the ability to teach.

Fifth, such frequent repetition of the same material will bring it about that even the slowest pupils may finally grasp the subject.

Thereby (sixth) everyone will make swifter and sounder progress in every respect.

And thus (seventh) every pupil will become a teacher, in some degree or other; consequently, the opportunities for multiplying knowledge will be mightily increased.

Then it will be clear how apt is the playful remark of Fortius: "I learned much from my teachers, more from my fellow-students, but most from my pupils." Or, as someone else has said, "The more often we impart learning, the more learned we become." Therein lies our enduring pleasure.[26]

160. These, then, are the fundamentals of the art of teaching, and from them can be derived infallible rules for the right teaching of all sciences and arts, liberal and mechanical, sacred and profane.[27]

26. Comenius writes this sentence in German: "Und so bleibet man immer bey der lust."

27. The concluding sentences of the chapter are put into this footnote because they merely serve to introduce chap. xi:

"We are now ready to make use of these principles and to evolve from them a didactics of languages. Here our fixed rule will be this:

"CLXXXVII. *Everything that is to constitute any part of the method of languages must conform to these didactic principles.*"

APPENDIXES

APPENDIX I

THE *MAGNA* AND THE *ANALYTICA*

In the second (Amsterdam) edition of the *Linguarum methodus novissima* Comenius introduces the tenth chapter (i.e., the *Analytical Didactic*) by calling attention to the analytical treatment of didactic principles therein; he also reminds us that his earlier work on method, the *Great Didactic*, had treated these principles syncritically. The principles enunciated in these two works sometimes agree and sometimes differ; furthermore, those of the *Analytical Didactic* are far more numerous than those of the *Great Didactic*. To facilitate comparison, I have extracted the axioms of the *Analytical Didactic* and placed them here side by side with the principles stated in chapters xvi–xxi of the *Great Didactic*. The syncritic method is best illustrated in chapters xvi–xix.

PRINCIPLES OF THE *GREAT DIDACTIC*
(Keatinge's Translation, II, 112–202)

CHAPTER XVI. THE UNIVERSAL REQUIREMENTS OF TEACHING
AND OF LEARNING

1. Nature observes a suitable time.
    We conclude, therefore, that
    i. The education of men should be commenced in the springtime of life, that is to say, in boyhood (for boyhood is the equivalent of spring, youth of summer, manhood of autumn, and old age of winter).
    ii. The morning hours are the most suitable for study (for here again the morning is the equivalent of spring, mid-day of summer, the evening of autumn, and the night of winter).
    iii. All the subjects that are to be learned should be arranged

so as to suit the age of the students, that nothing which is beyond their comprehension be given them to learn.

2. Nature prepares the material, before she begins to give it form.

It follows, therefore, that in order to effect a thorough improvement in schools it is necessary:

 i. That books and the materials necessary for teaching be held in readiness.

 ii. That the understanding be first instructed in things, and then taught to express them in language.

 iii. That no language be learned from a grammar, but from suitable authors.

 iv. That the knowledge of things precede the knowledge of their combinations.

 v. And that examples come before rules.

3. Nature chooses a fit subject to act upon, or first submits one to a suitable treatment in order to make it fit.

It is therefore desirable:

 i. That all who enter schools persevere in their studies.

 ii. That, before any special study is introduced, the minds of the students be prepared and made receptive of it.

 iii. That all obstacles be removed out of the way of schools.

4. Nature is not confused in its operations, but in its forward progress advances distinctly from one point to another.

Schools, therefore, should be organized in such a manner that the scholar shall be occupied with only one object of study at any given time.

5. In all the operations of nature development is from within.

It therefore follows

 i. That the scholar should be taught first to understand things, and then to remember them, and that no stress should be laid on the use of speech or pen, till after a training on the first two points.

 ii. That the teacher should know all the methods by which the understanding may be sharpened, and should put them into practice skilfully.

6. Nature, in its formative processes, begins with the universal and ends with the particular.

   i. Each language, science, or art must be first taught in its most simple elements, that the student may obtain a general idea of it.

   ii. His knowledge may next be developed further by placing rules and examples before him.

   iii. Then he may be allowed to learn the subject systematically with the exceptions and irregularities; and

   iv. last of all, may be given a commentary, though only where it is absolutely necessary. For he who has thoroughly mastered a subject from the beginning will have little need of a commentary, but will soon be in the position to write one himself.

7. Nature makes no leaps, but proceeds step by step.

   It follows therefore

   i. That all studies should be carefully graduated throughout the various classes, in such a way that those that come first may prepare the way for and throw light on those that come after.

   ii. That the time should be carefully divided, so that each year, each month, each day, and each hour may have its appointed task.

   iii. That the division of the time and of the subjects of study should be rigidly adhered to, that nothing may be omitted or perverted.

8. If nature commence anything, it does not leave off until the operation is completed.

   It follows therefore

   i. That he who is sent to school must be kept there until he becomes well informed, virtuous, and pious.

   ii. That the school must be situated in a quiet spot, far from noise and distractions.

   iii. That whatever has to be done, in accordance with the scheme of study, must be done without any shirking.

   iv. That no boys, under any pretext whatever, should be allowed to stay away or to play truant.

9. Nature carefully avoids obstacles and things likely to cause hurt.

> Care should therefore be taken
>
> i. That scholars receive no books but those suitable for their classes.
>
> ii. That these books be of such a kind that they can rightly be termed sources of wisdom, virtue, and piety.
>
> iii. That neither in the school nor in its vicinity the scholars be allowed to mix with bad companions.

CHAPTER XVII. THE PRINCIPLES OF FACILITY IN TEACHING AND IN LEARNING

1. Nature begins by a careful selection of materials.
2. Nature prepares its material so that it actually strives to attain the form.
3. Nature develops everything from beginnings which, though insignificant in appearance, possess great potential strength.
4. Nature advances from what is easy to what is more difficult.
5. Nature does not overburden herself, but is content with a little.
6. Nature does not hurry, but advances slowly.
7. Nature compels nothing to advance that is not driven forward by its own mature strength.
8. Nature assists its operations in every possible manner.
9. Nothing is produced by nature of which the practical application is not soon evident.
10. Nature is uniform in all its operations.

> Following in the footsteps of nature we find that the process of education will be easy
>
> i. If it begin early, before the mind is corrupted.
>
> ii. If the mind be duly prepared to receive it.
>
> iii. If it proceed from the general to the particular.
>
> iv. And from what is easy to what is more difficult.
>
> v. If the pupil be not overburdened by too many subjects.
>
> vi. And if progress be slow in every case.
>
> vii. If the intellect be forced to nothing to which its natural

bent does not incline it, in accordance with its age and with the right method.

viii. If everything be taught through the medium of the senses.

ix. And if the use of everything taught be continually kept in view.

x. If everything be taught according to one and the same method.

CHAPTER XVIII. THE PRINCIPLES OF THOROUGHNESS IN
TEACHING AND IN LEARNING

1. Nature produces nothing that is useless.
2. When bodies are being formed, nature omits nothing that is necessary for their production.
3. Nature does not operate on anything, unless it possess a foundation or roots.
4. Nature strikes her roots deep.
5. Nature develops everything from its roots and from no other source.
6. The more the uses to which nature applies anything, the more distinct subdivisions that thing will possess.
7. Nature never remains at rest, but advances continually; never begins anything afresh at the expense of work already in hand but proceeds with what she has begun, and brings it to completion.
8. Nature knits everything together in continuous combination.
9. Nature preserves a due proportion between the roots and the branches, with respect to both quality and quantity.
10. Nature becomes fruitful and strong through constant movement.

This [thorough and lasting knowledge] will be possible:

i. If only those subjects that are of real use be taken in hand.

ii. If these be taught without digression or interruption.

iii. If a thorough grounding precede instruction in detail.

iv. If this grounding be carefully given.

    v. If all that follows be based on this grounding, and on nothing else.

   vi. If, in every subject that consists of several parts, these parts be linked together as much as possible.

  vii. If all that comes later be based on what has gone before.

 viii. If great stress be laid on the points of resemblance between cognate subjects.

   ix. If all studies be arranged with reference to the intelligence and memory of the pupils, and the nature of language.

    x. If knowledge be fixed in the memory by constant practice.

CHAPTER XIX. THE PRINCIPLES OF CONCISENESS AND RAPIDITY IN TEACHING

1. The sun does not occupy itself with any single object, animal, or tree; but lights and warms the whole earth at once.

2. It gives light to all things with the same rays; covers all things with moisture by the same processes of evaporation and condensation; it causes the same wind to blow on all things; it puts all things in motion by the same warmth and cold.

3. It causes spring, summer, autumn, and winter to make their appearance in all lands at the same time. At the same time, through its agency, the trees grow green, blossom, and bear fruit (though naturally some do so earlier than others).

4. It always preserves the same order; one day resembles another, one year resembles the next. It always operates on one object by the same method.

5. It produces everything from its elementary form, and from no other source.

6. It produces in combination everything that ought to be combined; wood with its bark and its core, a flower with its leaves, a fruit with its skin and its stalk.

7. It causes everything to develop through definite stages, so

that one stage prepares the way for the next, and each stage follows naturally from the previous one.

8. Finally, it brings into existence nothing that is useless, or destroys such an object if it be accidentally produced.

In imitation of this

i. There should only be one teacher in each school, or at any rate in each class.

ii. Only one author should be used for each subject studied.

iii. The same exercise should be given to the whole class.

iv. All subjects and languages should be taught by the same method.

v. Everything should be taught thoroughly, briefly, and pithily, that the understanding may be, as it were, unlocked by one key, and may then unravel fresh difficulties of its own accord.

vi. All things that are naturally connected ought to be taught in combination.

vii. Every subject should be taught in definitely graded steps, that the work of one day may thus expand that of the previous day, and lead up to that of the morrow.

viii. And finally, everything that is useless should be invariably discarded.

CHAPTER XX. THE METHOD OF THE SCIENCES SPECIFICALLY

(Fourteen paragraphs of epistemological and "psychological" argument introduce the nine precepts listed below.)

1. Whatever is to be known must be taught.

2. Whatever is taught should be taught as being of practical application in every-day life and of some definite use.

3. Whatever is taught should be taught straightforwardly, and not in a complicated manner.

4. Whatever is taught must be taught with references to its true nature and its origin; that is to say, through its causes.

5. If anything is to be learned, its general principles must first be explained. Its details may then be considered, and not till then.

6. All the parts of an object, even the smallest, and without a single exception, must be learned with references to their order, their position, and the connection with one another.
7. All things must be taught in due succession, and not more than one thing should be taught at one time.
8. We should not leave any subject until it is thoroughly understood.
9. Stress should be laid on the differences which exist between things, in order that what knowledge of them is acquired may be clear and distinct.

CHAPTER XXI. THE METHOD OF THE ARTS

1. What has to be done must be learned by practice.
2. A definite model of that which has to be made must always be provided.
3. The use of instruments should be shown in practice and not by words; that is to say, by example rather than by precept.
4. Practice should commence with the rudiments and not with ambitious works.
5. Beginners should at first practise on a material that is familiar to them.
6. At first the prescribed form should be imitated with exactness. Later on more freedom may be allowed.
7. The models of the objects that have to be produced must be as perfect as is possible, so that if any one exercise himself sufficiently in imitating them it will be possible for him to become perfect in his art.
8. The first attempt at imitation should be as accurate as possible, that not the smallest deviation from the model be made.
9. Errors must be corrected by the master on the spot; but precepts, that is to say the rules, and the exceptions to the rules, must be given at the same time.
10. The perfect teaching of art is based on synthesis and analysis.
11. These exercises must be continued until artistic production becomes second nature.

AXIOMS OF THE *ANALYTICAL DIDACTIC*

I. GENERAL DIDACTICS

I. There is no knowledge without an idea or original image.

II. There is no knowledge except through the transformation of ideas into images.

III. There is no knowledge without an instrument of representation or means of image-making.

IV. We do not learn what we already know.

V. We learn the unknown only through the known.

VI. We learn the unknown only by learning.

VII. A student must always beware of learning anything badly.

VIII. Even a cautious student finds it impossible to avoid error at first.

IX. A student can become proficient only by degrees.

X. Therefore, a student always needs someone to guide him, admonish him, and correct him.

XI. Where no one teaches, nothing is taught.

XII. Where no one learns, nothing is learned.

XIII. Where there is no instruction, there is no transplanting of knowledge.

XIV. Teacher and student are complemental; neither can be absent from the act of teaching.

XV. The bond between teacher and student is instruction, as it passes from one to the other.

XVI. A good teacher, a good student, and good instruction increase knowledge mightily.

XVII. A teacher should be competent to teach (a learned teacher).

XVIII. A teacher should be skilful in teaching (a capable teacher).

XIX. A teacher should be zealous in teaching (a teacher to whom indolence and distaste are unknown).

XX. You will teach nothing to one who is incapable of being taught.

XXI. You will find it difficult to teach one who is unripe for instruction.

XXII. You will teach in vain one who is uninterested, unless you first make him eager for learning.

XXIII. Aptitude, discernment, and diligence, if present together, make for remarkable progress.

XXIV. Lack of aptitude or discernment must be compensated for by diligence.

XXV. Where there is neither aptitude nor discernment nor diligence, teaching and learning prosper little or not at all.

XXVI. Where nothing is taught, there nothing is learned.

XXVII. Where teaching is confused, there learning is confused.

XXVIII. Where teaching is careless, there learning is careless.

XXIX. Do not undertake to teach one who is not ready to be taught.

XXX. Do not postpone the instruction of one who is ready to receive it.

XXXI. Do not undertake to give instruction unless it commends itself to the pupil.

XXXII. Do not undertake to instruct a pupil unless his appetite has been keenly whetted.

XXXIII. Do not undertake instruction unless the pupil is equipped for the task.

XXXIV. The student should work and the teacher should direct.

XXXV. Where there is nothing to imitate (i.e., a model), there is no imitation.

XXXVI. Where there is no guidance (i.e., precept), imitation is neither easy nor certain.

XXXVII. Where there is no imitation (i.e., use, practice, exercises), guidance for imitation and even models are useless.

XXXVIII. The task of the teacher is to present the model, explain it, and show how to imitate it; the task of the student is to pay attention, comprehend, and imitate.

XXXIX. Without examples, precepts, and exercises, nothing is taught or learned unless it be incorrectly.

XL. All things are taught and learned through examples, precepts, and exercises.

XLI. The exemplar should always come first, the precept should always follow, and imitation should always be insisted upon.

XLII. We can best demonstrate how to do a thing by doing it.

XLIII. The virtue of a rule is that it be brief in words, clear in meaning, and full of truth.

XLIV. Rules are more useful if we employ them in conjunction with a task rather than apart from it, because in this way the student's errors give us an opportunity to repeat the rules and inculcate them anew.

XLV. Teacher and student should be mutually attentive.

XLVI. The student should follow the teacher at every turn, and the teacher should ever lead the way.

XLVII. Whenever the teacher sees the student deviating into error, he should admonish and instruct the student to follow in his footsteps more heedfully.

XLVIII. All parts of instruction should be coherent.

XLIX. One topic should not be abandoned for another unless the first has been mastered.

L. Later topics should be an occasion for the review of earlier ones.

LI. Without discipline one learns nothing or at least nothing correctly.

LII. Discipline should be constant, never slackening; it should always be treated seriously, never in jest.

LIII. Discipline should never be harsh.

LIV. Discipline should be of various levels.

LV. The bad is learned more easily than the good.

LVI. To learn is easier than to unlearn.

LVII. It is (likewise) easier to teach than to unteach.

LVIII. Teach nothing that a pupil must unlearn.

LIX. If a pupil has acquired any wrong knowledge, he should unlearn it as soon as possible.

LX. Since all things are more difficult to unlearn than to learn, we should see to it that there is no need to unlearn anything; we can achieve this in no other way than by taking the precaution not to add bad things to our knowledge or not to learn good things badly.

LXI. We learn easy things more easily, difficult ones with greater difficulty.

LXII. In the mass of subjects to be learned, some are always easier than others.

LXIII. Therefore (in the mass of subjects to be learned) we should always begin with the easier and proceed to the more difficult.

LXIV. We must always begin with the few, the brief, the simple, the general, the near, the regular, and proceed gradually to the more numerous, the more extensive, the more complex, the more particular, the more remote, the more irregular.

LXV. The few before the many.

LXVI. The brief before the long.

LXVII. The simple before the complex.

LXVIII. The general before the particular.

LXIX. The nearer before the more remote.

LXX. The regular before the irregular (or the analogous before the anomalous).

LXXI. Whatever can be taught and learned in one procedure should never be subdivided.

LXXII. Whatever is numerous should be gathered into wholes; the larger wholes should be analyzed first, then the smaller ones.

LXXIII. Whatever is long should be broken up into well-defined parts, and each part should be taken up in due order.

LXXIV. Whatever is complex should be resolved into its elements, and these should be learned first (in practice they should be performed first).

LXXV. Individual members should be gathered into kinds, kinds into classes, and classes into a general class. Then, whatever is equally true of all members we may assert about the whole class; on the other hand, whatever differences arise among the various kinds we may indicate for each kind separately, until we come (if need be) to the individual members.

LXXVI. Whatever is remote must be approached by steps so carefully chosen that the last step is clearly related to the first by an uninterrupted connection.

LXXVII. Every anomaly should be referred to some analogy by way of subordination.

LXXVIII. To know a thing, we must understand it.

LXXIX. To esteem a thing, we must understand it and choose it.

LXXX. To accomplish a thing, we must understand it, choose it, and perform it.

II. Special Methods

A. THE METHOD OF IMPLANTING KNOWLEDGE

LXXXI. No one knows anything (in the historical sense) except what he has learned.

LXXXII. All our knowledge comes by way of the senses, reason, and communication.

LXXXIII. The senses are the primary and the constant guides of knowledge.

LXXXIV. The senses are the solid foundations of knowledge.

LXXXV. We should observe everything with as many senses as possible.

LXXXVI. We should see to it that whatever has been presented to the senses is also understood.

LXXXVII. We should consider whether that which has been understood is right and fitting.

LXXXVIII. We should make sure that whatever has been understood and appraised sticks in the mind permanently.

LXXXIX. To know the differences between things is to know those things.

XC. To know the causes of things is to know the essence of things.

XCI. We must see to it that what we teach is clearly true.

XCII. We must make sure that what we teach is heeded attentively.

XCIII. We must take care that what we teach is first understood as a whole, then part by part, each part being distinct and in its place.

XCIV. Attempt only one thing at a time.

XCV. Always begin with the whole, then attempt the larger parts, and, finally, the details, one after another.

XCVI. Dwell on each part as long as it is necessary.

XCVII. We become acquainted with the parts of anything by means of analysis.

XCVIII. We come to know them more completely if we also employ synthesis.

XCIX. We come to know them most completely if, in addition, we employ syncrisis.

C. When we seek exact knowledge of things, we must combine the analytic, synthetic, and syncritic methods.

CI. To know the exemplars of things is the foundation of judgment.

CII. To compare things with their exemplars is the act of judgment.

CIII. To compare things with their exemplars rightly

and then to pronounce a right opinion is the completion of judgment.

CIV. We should establish the universal forms and norms of things and show how they guide us in dealing with each particular thing.

CV. What you wish to remember, first imprint in the memory.

CVI. The more permanently you wish to remember anything or the more readily you wish to recall it, the more deeply you must imprint it in the memory.

CVII. Strength of memory derives primarily from strength of impression.

CVIII. Aids to perception, understanding, and judgment are also aids to memory.

CIX. Whatever does not make sense can be neither understood nor appraised and hence cannot be committed to memory.

CX. Whatever lacks coherence is difficult to understand and to judge; for the same reason it is also difficult to commit to memory.

CXI. Just as order in things is the basis of understanding and judgment, so also is it the basis of memory.

CXII. When particulars are lacking, it is almost impossible to understand or judge a matter and equally impossible to commit it to memory.

CXIII. First impressions are lasting.

CXIV. Impressions received through heedful observation are very lasting.

CXV. Impressions received by a mind affected by emotion are deep and lasting.

CXVI. The best impressions are gained direct from things themselves.

CXVII. Leisurely reflection fixes the impression of an object.

CXVIII. To retrace an impression is to strengthen it.

CXIX. To probe and test an impression is to reinforce it.

CXX. Repetition is an antidote against forgetfulness.

CXXI. Writing is a storehouse of repetition.

CXXII. Symbolic representation of things is the key and the keystone of memory.

CXXIII. Comprehension, of whatever kind, is the light of memory.

CXXIV. Partition of the unlimited is a great instrument of memory.

CXXV. Recollection depends on occasion.

CXXVI. Occasions for recollection are linked as in a chain.

CXXVII. The occasion or starting point of recollection should be the known; the object of recollection should be the less known.

B. THE METHOD OF TEACHING PRUDENCE

CXXVIII. To understand rightly what is beneficial and what is harmful constitutes the basis of prudence.

CXXIX. To choose the beneficial and to avoid the harmful constitutes the act of prudence.

CXXX. To make indifferent use of what is indifferent constitutes a supplement to prudence.

C. THE METHOD OF WORKS

CXXXI. Let theory always come before practice.

CXXXII. Let prudence always accompany practice.

CXXXIII. Let practice always bring practice to perfection.

CXXXIV. When a pupil is to perform something, present him with an exemplar, show him the implements, and teach him how to imitate.

CXXXV. A beginner is never to be relied upon and for that reason should be watched lest he fall into error.

CXXXVI. In every art there should be more practice than theory.

CXXXVII. Practice should begin with the smallest, not with the largest; with parts, not with the whole; with rudiments, not with the finished works.

D. THE METHOD OF LANGUAGES

CXXXVIII. The teacher should teach not as much as he himself can teach but as much as the learner can grasp.

CXXXIX. The first age should be instructed only in matters that touch the senses.

CXL. The first age should be well instructed in matters that touch the senses.

CXLI. The first age should be trained chiefly in those studies which depend on the use of the memory.

CXLII. Pupils of maturer age should be introduced to the causes of things.

CXLIII. To penetrate to the true causes of many things is to arrive at a pure understanding of things.

CXLIV. Either the teacher should be not excessively talented or he should be schooled in patience.

CXLV. The teacher should stoop to the level of the pupil and assist his power of comprehension in every way possible.

CXLVI. The negligence of a pupil must be offset by the diligence of the teacher.

CXLVII. The training of the untrained should begin with the rudiments.

CXLVIII. The training of those who are beginning to make progress should proceed gradually.

CXLIX. Let beginners perform not many things but much of one thing; let those who are continuing or completing their studies perform not so much of one thing as a variety of things.

CL. Beginners should work strictly according to models; more advanced pupils should work without models in front of them; accomplished students should work independently.

CLI. Let beginners work slowly, advanced pupils somewhat faster, and accomplished students very fast.

CLII. Let the training of a faulty worker begin with the removal of the fault.

CLIII. A partial task is desultory, depends on circumstances, and requires no rules.

CLIV. Perfect instruction must be erected on its own foundations; these should be so ample that the whole structure of teaching can be developed from them, and they should be so solid that all parts can stand through their own strength without the need of outside support.

CLV. He who learns in the popular way must take things on faith; he who learns as an expert must seek out reasons.

CLVI. Expert knowledge begins in sense-perception and ends in comprehension when reason is the intermediary.

CLVII. Therefore, human talent should be trained in such a way that these steps are not confused.

[CLVIII. If your allotted time is strictly limited, you should perform nothing except that for which there is utmost need.]

III. Special Memoranda on How To Teach Rapidly, Agreeably, and Thoroughly

CLVIII. Rapidity is greatly promoted by constant examples, agreeableness by clear precepts, and thoroughness by continual practice.

A. Concerning Rapidity

CLIX. Straight to the mark; avoid all bypaths.

CLX. When few means suffice to accomplish anything, no need to use more.

CLXI. All means should be ready and at hand.

CLXII. Always gradually, never by leaps and bounds.

CLXIII. Always treat related matters together.

CLXIV. Unbroken progression makes for notable progress.

CLXV. Uniformity in method makes for rapidity in learning.

B. CONCERNING AGREEABLENESS

CLXVI. We must do our utmost to guard against aversion, the most insidious poison in studies.

CLXVII. To deal with aptitudes as their nature demands is the basis of agreeable progress.

CLXVIII. The teacher should never be morose in the discharge of his duties but should perform all of them with paternal kindness.

CLXIX. Let the course of every study be as brief and as well organized as possible.

CLXX. We must attract our pupils by constantly appealing to their senses.

CLXXI. Let everything be learned through individual practice.

CLXXII. Let everything be learned for use.

CLXXIII. Whatever is taught should be tempered by pleasing variety.

CLXXIV. Whatever is studied should be studied by several pupils at the same time and under some pleasant form of rivalry.

C. CONCERNING THOROUGHNESS OF INSTRUCTION

CLXXV. Where solid instruction is required, we must reject trivial subjects and matters whose truth or usefulness cannot be demonstrated.

CLXXVI. Everything with gusto.

CLXXVII. Examples should be selected for the distinctness with which they expose the subject to view, so that no part of it remains obscure. Precepts, on the other hand, should be few, clear, and universally true so that they may be safely trusted. Lastly, exercises should be patterned on an examplar until they express it to the life.

CLXXVIII. At the beginning everything should be of the very best: models, rules, attention, and, finally, the teacher himself.

CLXXIX. All beginnings should be slow but accurate: attention, perception, and, finally, imitation.

CLXXX. Unless the first layers have been firmly established, nothing new should be erected upon them.

CLXXXI. Everything fully, from end to end and through all intermediate parts.

CLXXXII. Everything to the core, through causes laid bare.

CLXXXIII. Everything through one's own senses, constantly and variously.

CLXXXIV. Everything through the constant practice of the students themselves.

CLXXXV. Let there be constant reviews and examinations.

CLXXXVI. Every pupil should acquire the habit of also acting as teacher.

CLXXXVII. Everything that is to constitute any part of the method of languages must conform to these didactic principles.

APPENDIX II

THE NEW METHOD AND ITS TEXTBOOKS

The *Methodus* was intended as an exposition of a theory and as a practical guide for the use of textbooks based on that theory. Since the *Analytica*, the tenth chapter of the *Methodus*, formulated a set of principles which demanded a new approach to the teaching of languages, Comenius rewrote and radically modified the *Vestibulum* of 1633 and the *Ianua* of 1631 in order to make them conform to the New Method. Chapters xiv and xv of the *Methodus* fully describe the new *Vestibulum* and *Ianua* and explain how these works are to be employed in the first two grades of instruction. Chapter xvi merely sketches a new work, the *Atrium*, which was intended for the third grade; and chapter xviii lists the desiderata in an anthology or course of readings which was to be the Palace or Treasury in the Comenian educational structure. Only the new *Vestibulum* and the new *Ianua* were completed when the *Methodus* was published.

Each of the four grades was to be supplied with a separate text, grammar, and lexicon; thus the completed series would have consisted of twelve major works. Comenius also planned and in part completed various subsidiary texts like the *Orbis pictus* and several *informatoria* or sets of instructions for teachers. The bibliographical history of the whole project is extremely complicated; indeed, in the light of our present knowledge some of the problems are insoluble.[1] The following table sums up the known history of the four grades of texts.

I. *a*) Original *Vestibulum*, written 1632–33; printed Leszno, 1633; reprinted in *ODO*, I, 302–17: *Ianuae linguarum reseratae vestibulum. S.l., s.a.*

   b) New *Vestibulum*, written 1643–49; Introduction and speci-

1. For a detailed discussion of these problems consult the Index in Novák-Hendrich.

mens reprinted in *ODO*, II, 293–98: *Vestibulum Latinae linguae, rerum et linguae cardines exhibens (ad leges methodi linguarum novissimae concinnatum)*. *S.l.*, *s.a.*

II. *a)* Original (Latin) *Ianua*, written 1629–31; printed Leszno, 1631; reprinted in *ODO*, I, 250–302: *Ianua linguarum reserata S.l.*, *s.a.*[2]

   b) New *Ianua*, written 1643–49; Introduction reprinted in *ODO*, II, 299–304: *Latinae linguae Ianua reserata, rerum et linguae structuram exhibens ordine nativo*. (*Ad leges methodi linguarum novissimae*.) Leszno, 1649.[3]

III. The *Atrium* intended for the Swedish schools was never completed, but Comenius during his stay at Sáros Pátak published one atrial text and began work on another:

   1. *Eruditionis scholasticae pars III: Atrium, rerum et linguarum ornamenta exhibens* (1652), reprinted in *ODO*, III, 451–718 (pagination confused).

   2. *Lexicon atriale Latino-Latinum* (Amsterdam, 1657), composed between 1650 and 1657.

IV. The Palace or Treasury is not found in any of Comenius' known works.[4]

The *Atrium* discussed in the *Methodus* replaces the *Palatium* of an earlier plan according to which Comenius had intended to construct a *Vestibulum*, a *Ianua*, a *Palatium*, and a *Thesaurus*. This earlier scheme is outlined in the *Dissertatio didactica* (Breslau, 1638) and in the *Didactica magna*, which, though not published until 1657, was composed between 1633 and 1638. The description of this earlier plan is given below in Keatinge's

2. Although first printed in Latin, the *Ianua* was originally written in Czech; the Czech version was published in Leszno under the title *Dvře jazyků otevřené* (1633). For a survey of the numerous editions, revisions, and adaptations of the Latin *Ianua* see Jan Kvačala, *Die pädagogische Reform des Comenius in Deutschland* (Berlin, 1904), II, 171 ff. (*Monumenta Germaniae pedagogica*, Vol. XXXII.)

3. The *Vestibulum* and *Ianua* when revised for Hungarian schools were published in 1652 as *Eruditionis scholasticae pars prima: Vestibulum* and *Eruditionis scholasticae pars II: Ianua*. This *Ianua* consists of a Latin-Magyar lexicon and little else.

4. See "Contents of the *Methodus*," n. 46, above.

translation, *The Great Didactic*, Volume II, chapter xxii, paragraphs 17–24:[5]

17. This course of language study may be divided into four ages—

			in which we learn to speak	
The first	age is	babbling infancy		indistinctly
The second		ripening boyhood		correctly
The third		maturer youth		elegantly
The fourth		vigorous manhood		forcibly

18. Gradation of this kind is the only true principle.

On any other system everything falls into confusion and disorder, as we have most of us experienced. But through these four grades all who wish to learn languages may pass with ease if the proper materials for teaching languages have been provided; that is to say, suitable schoolbooks for the pupils and handbooks to assist the teacher, both of which should be short and methodical.

19. The schoolbooks, suited to the several ages, should be four in number: (i) the *Vestibulum;* (ii) the *Janua;* (iii) the *Palatium;* and (iv) the *Thesaurus.*

20. The *Vestibulum* should contain the materials for a child's conversation—a few hundred words, arranged in sentences, to which are added the declensions of nouns and the conjugations of verbs.

21. The *Janua* should contain all the common words in the language, about eight thousand in number. These should be arranged in short sentences embodying descriptions of natural objects. To this there should be subjoined some short and clear grammatical rules, giving accurate directions for writing, pronouncing, forming, and using the words of the language.

22. The *Palatium* should contain diverse discourses on all matters, expressed in a varied and elegant style, with marginal references to the authors from which the several phrases are borrowed. At the end there should be given rules for altering and paraphrasing sentences in a thousand different ways.

5. The general plan of the New Method is outlined in chap. xii of the *Methodus;* see Introduction, pp. 58–61, above.

23. The *Thesaurus* will be the name given to the classic writers who have written on any matter with serious intent and in a good style, with the addition of rules relating to the observation and collection of noteworthy passages and to the accurate translation (a most important matter) of idioms. Of these authors, some should be chosen to read in school; of others, a catalogue should be formed, so that, if anyone desires to look up any subject in the authors who have written on it, he may be able to find out who they are.

24. By subsidiary books are meant those by whose help the schoolbooks may be used with greater speed and with more result.

For the *Vestibulum* a small vocabulary, both vernacular-Latin and Latin-vernacular, should be provided.

For the *Janua* an etymological Latin-vernacular dictionary, giving the simple words, their derivatives, their compounds, and the reason for the meanings attached.

For the *Palatium* a phraseological dictionary in the vernacular, in Latin (and if necessary in Greek), forming a compendium of the various phrases, synonyms, and periphrases that occur in the *Palatium*, with references to places where they are to be found.

Finally, for the completion of the *Thesaurus*, a comprehensive lexicon (vernacular-Latin and Latin-Greek) which shall embrace, without exception, every point in each language. This should be carried out in a scholarly and accurate manner, care being taken that fine shades of meaning in the several languages be made to correspond and that suitable parallels be found for idoms. For it is not probable that there exists any language so poor in words, idioms, and proverbs that it could not furnish an equivalent for any Latin expression, if judgment were used. At any rate, accurate renderings could be devised by anyone who possessed sufficient skill in imitating and in producing a suitable result from suitable material.

APPENDIX III

THE HALLE MANUSCRIPTS

In 1935 Professor Čyževskij discovered in the archives of the Waisenhaus in Halle a.d. Saale five Latin works of Comenius which for almost three centuries had been considered lost. A full account of these discoveries was not published until 1940.[1] Up to the present time no edition of the original Latin texts has appeared, but before his death in 1950 Josef Hendrich was able to complete Czech translations of two of the newly discovered works, the *Pampaedia* and the *Panorthosia*.[2] Thus the irony that pervaded the life of Comenius enjoys a posthumous career. Comenius began his literary activities by writing for his countrymen in Czech, but, in order to reach a larger audience, he adopted Latin as the language of his most important and most voluminous works. Now the long-lost Latin texts of what he considered his great contribution to human welfare are made available to the public not in the original Latin but in modern Czech.

The Halle manuscripts contain Parts III–VII of Comenius' "General Consultation about the Improvement of Human Affairs," the Latin title of which reads: *De rerum humanarum emendatione Consultatio catholica ad genus humanum, ante alios vero ad eruditos, religiosos, potentes Europae.* Although Comenius labored on this work from about 1645 until his death in 1670, only the Dedication and the first two parts were printed during his lifetime.[3] This one-volume publication contains an elaborate

1. Dimitri Čyževskij, "Hallské rukopisy děl J. A. Komenského," *Archiv pro bádání o životě a spisech J. A. Komenského*, No. 15 (Brno, 1940), pp. 85 ff.

2. The *Pampaedia* under the title *Vševýchova* (Praha, 1948) and the *Panorthosia* under the title *Všenáprava* (Praha, 1950).

3. In 1662 or perhaps as early as 1656, without indication of time or place of publication; cf. Novák-Hendrich, p. 697, and *Continuatio admonitionis* (1669), Sec. 122.

Dedication, the *Panegersia* (Part I of the *Consultatio*), and the *Panaugia* (Part II), each with a separate title-page.

The Dedication, addressed to learned, devout, and eminent men, the "lights of Europe" (*Europae luminibus*), outlines the general plan of the *Consultatio* and indicates how the author will treat his subject in seven parts:

I. *Panegersia* ("Universal Awakening"). This introductory work defines human affairs in terms of education, polity, and religion. It will therefore be the author's task to survey three kinds of human relationship: (1) the relations of man to things, over which he should exercise sovereignty; (2) the relations of man to his fellow-men, with whom he should live on reasonable terms, in amity and in peace; and (3) the relations of man to God, to whom man should be ever submissive, bending his will to the will of God so as to prepare himself for an eternal sojourn with God. The author shows that it is possible to make these relationships conform to the will of God but that humanity has failed to do so and consequently has brought its own affairs to a state of utter confusion. He then ponders the question whether some amendment of mankind's affairs is not possible and whether by arousing pity for human misery and kindling a desire for the betterment of man's lot he cannot bring about a Universal Awakening (*Excitatorium universale*).

II. *Panaugia* ("Universal Dawning"). Here the author traces the ways in which the general Awakening can be brought about. He concludes that the one great force capable of banishing darkness from the human mind is the light of all-penetrating thought. This is the way of Universal Light (*Lucis universalis via*) which leads to a Universal Dawning.

III. *Pantaxia* ("Universal Correlation"), which the author formerly had named *Pansophia* ("Universal Wisdom" or "Universal Knowledge").[4] This part shows how the universal light of thought enables us to classify all things and assign each thing to its proper place. By making our thinking conform to things as they are, we create an unbreakable chain of thought corresponding to the great chain of being. In this way we achieve a coherent

4. In the Halle manuscripts this work is entitled *Pansophia*.

and steady view of creation whereby we perceive the true nature, order, and manner of all phenomena. This is the task of the Universal Co-ordination or Correlation of Things (*Rerum universalis coordinatio*).

IV. *Pampaedia* ("Universal Education"). In order to teach everyone how to comprehend the essential correlation of all things, we must discover how the human mind can be made to grasp the Universal Light. Universal Education will therefore explore the problems of the Universal Cultivation of Minds (*Universalis cultura mentium*).

V. *Panglottia* ("Universal Language Study"). The fifth book will attempt to discover the means of spreading the Universal Light and of making it penetrate all nations and races. Since intellectual enlightenment can be conveyed only in the vehicle of language, this work will devote itself to the problem of the Universal Cultivation of Languages (*Linguarum universalis cultura*).

VI. *Panorthosia* ("Universal Reform"). By virtue of the reforms outlined in the preceding books we should be able to bring about reforms in educational, religious, and civic affairs. To show how we can inaugurate an age of enlightenment, piety, and peace is the function of this sixth book, which deals with Universal Reform (*Reformatio universalis*).

VII. *Pannuthesia* ("Universal Admonition"). When the feasibility of these proposals has been established, all educated men, all religious thinkers, and all the potentates of the world, indeed, all Christians, should be exhorted to occupy themselves seriously with these weighty matters and to devote themselves to the task of making these plans a reality. This call to action will be a Universal Admonition and Exhortation (*Exhortatorium universale*).

Before 1935 it was believed that the Dedication, the *Panegersia*, and the *Panaugia*, all three of which had been published by Comenius himself, were the only extant parts of the *Consultatio*. The five other parts, which had been prepared for publication after the death of Comenius by Christian Nigrin and Paul Hartmann, were ready for the press by the end of 1678 but

were never printed. Nothing is known of these texts. Around
the year 1700, however, all the materials for an edition of the
Consultatio came into the possession of Justus Docemius, who
intrusted them to the care of the Waisenhaus in Halle. These materials were used by Budde for his edition of the *Panegersia* in
1702, but after that year all trace of them disappeared until
they were recovered by Čyževskij. Before these "lost" works
were discovered in 1935, their content had been broadly sur-
mised from other Comenian writings on pansophy and from
contemporary references in diaries and correspondence. Valuable evidence was also supplied by the polemical writings of
Maresius, who published in 1669 a series of abusive but detailed
criticisms of the chiliastic and irenic proposals in the *Panorthosia*, parts of which Comenius had published for a small circle
of critics.[5] Hence careful inference and brilliant conjecture were
able to reconstruct the general outlines of the *Consultatio*. But
now, with the discovery of the Halle materials, which consist not
only of manuscripts but also of some printed sheets, the actual
texts of all seven parts are available, although the five previously
unknown texts still remain unpublished. The various parts of
the *Consultatio* as we now have them are listed in the following
table.

A. ONE VOLUME PRINTED DURING THE LIFETIME OF COMENIUS

De rerum humanarum emendatione CONSULTATIO CATHOLICA ad
genus humanum, ante alios vero ad eruditos, religiosos, potentes
Europae ("General Consultation about the Improvement of Human
Affairs [addressed] to Humankind, above All to the Learned, Religious,
and Powerful Men of Europe").

I. De emendatione rerum humanarum consultationis catholicae
pars prima, PANEGERSIA, EXCITATORIUM UNIVERSALE ("Pan-

5. Samuel Des Marets (Maresius) engaged in various controversies with
Comenius; his most detailed attack upon the chiliastic and irenic chapters
of the *Panorthosia* is to be found in a book, the charming title of which reflects the *odium theologicum* of seventeenth-century polemical writings:
*Antirrheticus, sive defensio pii zeli pro retinenda recepta in ecclesiis reformatis
doctrina, praesertim adversus chiliastas et fanaticos; contra Joh. A. Comenii
fanatici zelum amarum, scientia et conscientia destitutum* (Groningen, 1669).

egersia, Universal Awakening, the First Part of the General Consultation about the Improvement of Human Affairs").

II. De rerum humanarum emendatione consultationis pars secunda, PANAUGIA ("Panaugia or Universal Dawning, the Second Part of the Consultation about the Improvement of Human Affairs").

B. HALLE MANUSCRIPTS DISCOVERED IN 1935

III. Humano generi communis liber PANSOPHIA, h.e. universalis sapientia, fundata super ipsam naturam ("A Book for All Humankind, Pansophia, i.e., Universal Wisdom Based upon Nature Itself").[6]

IV. De rerum humanarum emendatione consultationis catholicae pars quarta PAMPAEDIA ("Pampaedia or Universal Education, the Fourth Part of the General Consultation about the Improvement of Human Affairs").

V. De rerum humanarum emendatione consultationis catholicae pars quinta PANGLOTTIA ("Panglottia or Universal Language Study, the Fifth Part of the General Consultation about the Improvement of Human Affairs").

VI. De rerum humanarum emendatione consultationis catholicae pars sexta PANORTHOSIA ("Panorthosia or Universal Reform, the Sixth Part of the General Consultation about the Improvement of Human Affairs").

VII. De rerum humanarum emendatione consultationis catholicae pars septima PANNUTHESIA ("Pannuthesia or Universal Admonition, the Seventh Part of the General Consultation about the Improvement of Human Affairs").

The *Consultatio* is Comenius' most ambitious work. Its author considered it his supreme contribution to the welfare of humanity; and we, whatever our estimate of its intrinsic worth, must reckon with it as the author's final and most elaborate disquisition on the pansophic, chiliastic, and irenic notions that guided and informed his life's work. No definitive study of the filiation of Comenius' thought in the *Didaktika*, the *Didactica magna*, and the *Didactica analytica* can be made until the framework of that thought has been clarified by an analysis of the whole *Consultatio*. We cannot pretend to define the scope and full intention of Comenian writings on education, and we cer-

6. In the Dedication this part is entitled *Pantaxia*.

tainly cannot arrive at any just estimate of Comenius' position in the intellectual history of Europe until the newly discovered parts of the *Consultatio* have been fully edited and carefully studied. We may deny the validity of the author's metaphysics, reject his ethical and religious assumptions, and doubt the value of his schemes and methods; or we may construe his dicta as arguments in an oligarchic, democratic, libertarian, or egalitarian dialectic.[7] But before we can understand the intellectual system of Comenius, before we can know "the furniture of his mind," we must have the opportunity of reading what he wrote

7. In recent years careful exegesis by Gončarov, Gruzděv, Kairov, Medynskij, and others has transformed Comenius into an apostle of Soviet educational theory.

INDEX

INDEX